CONSCIOUS
MILLIONAIRE

CONSCIOUS
MILLIONAIRE

GROW YOUR
BUSINESS BY
Making a Difference

JV CRUM, III

Conscious World Press

Books may be purchased in quantity by contacting the publisher directly at:
www.ConsciousWorldPress.com | info@ConsciousWorldPress.com | 888-818-0816

Publisher: Conscious World Press, LLC
Editor: LinDee Rochelle
Designer: Rebecca Finkel

ISBN paperback: 978-0-9767192-2-9
ISBN hard cover: 978-0-9767192-5-0
ISBN e-Book: 978-0-9767192-4-3
Library of Congress Catalogue Number 2013921258

Shelf Categories: 1. Entrepreneur 2. Business

Printed in the USA

Conscious Millionaire is dedicated to my parents:

My mother, Gwendolyn Randolph Ramage Crum,
an educator who inspired me and thousands
of others to awaken our potential
and achieve at our highest;

My father, James "Jim" Vivien Crum II,
a friend who taught me life values,
a leader who constantly gave to others,
and a man who was, above all else,
a true Southern Gentleman.

A portion of the sales of this book
supports the efforts of the non-profit
Conscious World Foundation Inc.,
including its youth leadership
trainings and annual global
Conscious World Day.

Please visit their site at:
ConsciousWorld.org

BOOK PURPOSE

My Purpose in writing this book and beginning the Conscious Millionaire Institute is to help you make a powerful difference by building a profitable business.

It is also to provide the path, tools, and support for at least one million entrepreneurs to become true Conscious Millionaires.

Will YOU become one of them?

CONTENTS

FOREWORD

Making a difference and transforming others has been at the core of my own work as the leader and CEO of the Money and You® Program. The purpose of our organization, *Excellerated Business Schools®* for Entrepreneurs, is to *Uplift Humanity's Consciousness through Business.*

J V's seminal book is a perfect companion to my work. It is in alignment with what we teach in our Money and You® Program. Through his work at the Conscious Millionaire® Institute, J V teaches his *Triple Win*™ principle: you, others, and society winning together. I feel as if I have found a "brother" in this man who is one of the transformational leaders of our time.

Like many successful entrepreneurs, J V was not born into wealth. He grew up in a small country town in a family that frequently struggled financially. In his twenties, he made his first million by stepping into a chaos-driven, family trucking company that was bleeding cash and on the edge of bankruptcy. By turning it around, then growing and ultimately selling it, he reaped the reward of his tenacity and insight.

Now you get that same insight and wisdom layered with additional years of building his own businesses and coaching other business owners. Through his book, he is your coach, mentor, and guide on a path that unites creating profits with achieving a higher purpose. J V seamlessly weaves these two motives throughout his book, which is designed to teach both new and seasoned entrepreneurs how to make their chosen difference in our world.

Today's entrepreneurs are no longer willing to compromise by only pursuing profits at the cost of not also having personal fulfillment and doing something they feel matters. There is a whole new generation of socially-minded entrepreneurs coming on line. These are the same entrepreneurs who seek the program we offer at the Excellerated Business Schools and the wisdom offered through Conscious Millionaire.

My mentors were pioneers in the field of transformational business teachings with the added dimension of Social Responsibility. Our mentor, the benevolent Dr. R. Buckminster Fuller, was named one of the Top 100 most influential persons of the 20th century by *Time Magazine*. He was a great futurist who proved through his work there really is enough to feed everyone on this planet, and that it is our obligation to create a world that works for everyone.

J V is one of the current day visionaries. His book embodies his wisdom, practical knowledge, and cutting edge insights. In it he provides a step-by-step path for entrepreneurs who seek to create change while building wealth.

Each of us has a responsibility to create our financial destinies. Through sound business principles, strategies, and the coaching found in each chapter of this visionary book, J V shows you how. This is a business book that gives the reader the entire range of what he or she needs to become successful in business. It not only provides result-based, bottom line strategies for making money, it also gives insights for how to access the deeper, authentic flow of life and connect with your own visionary consciousness.

Read, study, and apply the *Formula for Creating Wealth*™ found in this book. Utilize it to make your financial decisions as you explore the infinite possibilities for how your business can change the lives of others and our world.

Welcome to a wonderful new paradigm. May you and the society in which we all live, prosper and thrive. Enjoy the journey of building your business and making your contribution as a Conscious Millionaire Entrepreneur.

Aloha!
DAME D C CORDOVA
CEO, Excellerated Business Schools® for Entrepreneurs,
Money and You® Program
www.Excellerated.com

INTRODUCTION

Conscious Millionaire is about consciously choosing your destiny and becoming empowered to create it. In this book, you will discover a new approach to business. Whether you are an entrepreneur, business owner, manager, leader, or someone seeking to start your first business, this book is a guide for how to consciously grow a business.

You probably picked up this book for three reasons. First, you want to grow a business that provides the level of financial success you desire. Second, like an increasing number of entrepreneurs, you desire to consciously create your wealth by making a difference. Third, you are seeking a path that will provide the time, freedom, and financial resources necessary for you to enjoy a fulfilled and happy life.

For entrepreneurially-minded men and women, the material can be utilized to start a private business as well as to create an entrepreneurial team within a larger organization. The formula, strategies, and principles in this book are applicable to any size business.

Moreover, it is your path for moving from *First Stage Capitalism™*, which only focuses on profit, to *Second Stage Capitalism™*, which combines making money with making a difference. Like all journeys, it begins wherever you are—right here and right now.

In addition to those who are traditionally thought of as entrepreneurs, you could have professional training or possess an expert skill that forms the heart of your entrepreneurial passion.

For example, you could be a speaker, coach, author, thought leader, healer, marketer, sales professional, or any other type of expert. You seek a conscious path for building your wealth that is honest, high integrity, and helps others.

Perhaps you currently own a business that provides the opportunity to do something you enjoy. Yet, you are struggling and frustrated because you don't generate consistent profits. You are searching for how to turn it around without giving up your values.

You may have a job and feel trapped between living your dreams and a weekly pay check. You want to start your own business. Yet, it's critical you make the right decisions because you can't afford to lose your money.

In *Conscious Millionaire*, you will discover how to free your mind from old beliefs and conventional wisdom about what is possible for your business and life. As this occurs, you will begin to awaken your potential and perform at profound, new levels.

The level of consciousness of the world is rising and more people feel an inner calling to do something that truly matters with their lives. Entrepreneurs increasingly desire to become a force for good in how they make money. They want to make a big difference.

Big differences are found in big dreams. What is *your* big dream? What are *you* passionate to accomplish? If anything was possible, how would your business help others and change our world? What would your larger business purpose be?

Before you answer these questions, take a moment right now to expand your consciousness of what is possible. Imagine that you have a clear vision of your ideal life and business. Envision a detailed picture of the difference you desire to make. Now visualize yourself moving forward, 100 percent confident you can accomplish anything.

Consider how much faster and easier you could become a millionaire entrepreneur if you knew the *Formula for Creating*

Wealth and possessed the secrets needed to apply it. Imagine these included how to maximize your results, choose the right team members, and achieve financial freedom consciously.

Now, become aware of how your consciousness quickly shifted—and expanded—as you visualized these new possibilities. Notice how much more empowered you feel now.

Throughout *Conscious Millionaire* you will find the strategies, insights, and tools that I've discovered during three decades of building and selling companies, coaching business clients, and observing what works best in the business world.

You are on Earth to achieve a greater good—and the *faster* you accomplish it, the better our world will become. That leads to another reason I wrote this book. I want to help you achieve in twelve months, what many entrepreneurs take years to accomplish.

The final reason I wrote this book and it is the one closest to my heart. I want to help you become a true Conscious Millionaire. I desire to support you accomplishing what I call the *Triple Win*: you, others, and society winning together.

As we both know, there are no accidents in life. You and I have actually understood this for some time. Out of all the books in the universe, you chose *Conscious Millionaire*. I believe it was for a reason. You are ready to enjoy abundant wealth and create a life of true significance.

I consider it an honor and privilege that you have chosen to pursue this journey with me. My sincere hope is that with each *conscious focused action* you take, both your bank account and your life will become richer.

Now it's time for YOU to become a Conscious Millionaire. Turn the page and let's get started...

Get The Most From *Conscious Millionaire*

To maximize your experience and help you rapidly move forward on your Conscious Millionaire Journey, I've included the following throughout:

1. QR CODES

If you haven't noticed these in newspapers, magazines, or marketing, they are Quick Response Codes, or QR Codes—which are similar to bar codes. You will find them throughout this book. They provide instant access to *bonus resources*, such as coaching videos, audios, or downloadable worksheets. To read the Codes, just download a free QR Reader from your smart phone's APP store. Then open it on your phone (or tablet), point your phone camera at the **QR Code to scan it**, and you will gain instant access to the Conscious Millionaire Membership site. *Note*: You don't have to use the QR Codes because there is also a ***link next to each code***.

Paste it into your browser or, if you have the E-book, just *click on the link*. **Try it now**.

 ConsciousMillionaire.com/member

2. Conscious Millionaire Coaching: At the end of each chapter, you will find the following: **(1) Build Your Strategy**, which teaches you how to utilize the *Formula for Creating Wealth* found in the book to develop a strategy that leverages the material in that chapter; **(2) Grow Your Business**, which contains three action items that will help you rapidly grow your business; **(3) Create Your Journey**, which has three suggestions for the order in which you may choose to read this book; and **(4) QR Codes / links**, which lead to bonus material located at our membership site.

3. Conscious Millionaire Journal: To help you get the most out of the coaching exercises, I've provided a journal for you to download from the membership site. Use the journal to complete the coaching exercises found in *Conscious Millionaire*. The journal also contains valuable bonus resources to help you build your business. You can either utilize it as a digital file, or print it and write in it manually. Use the QR Code/ link above to access the membership site and download your free *Conscious Millionaire Journal* now.

SPECIAL READER BONUS

As a special bonus to help you get the most from this book, enjoy 30 days Free access to the Conscious Millionaire Membership Site. At the site, there are over fifteen coaching videos and audios designed to provide additional insights for how to best use the material in each chapter. You will also find:

- *Expert Interviews* on how to consciously grow your business and increase profits quickly;

- *Training Calls* on each of the monthly topics;

- *Behind-the-Scenes Videos* of J V Crum III discussing his latest business strategies and insights; and

- *The Millionaire Blog* with exclusive "member only" blogs and articles.

The membership site is *free* for 30 days as a gift to you. Access it to download your *Conscious Millionaire Journal* now.

 ConsciousMillionaire.com/member

Note: All QR Codes and links are guaranteed to work through December 31, 2016.

CHAPTER 1

YOUR MILLIONAIRE JOURNEY

If you miss your real journey,
you miss your real life.

I was twenty-five years old and had just moved into my beautiful home on Bayshore Boulevard, the "Fifth Avenue" of Tampa, Florida. My home overlooked the scenic Tampa Bay. Imagine the view: palm trees blowing in the wind, sailboats moving on the bay, and water stretching out as far as the eye could see. The garage was occupied with my Mercedes which welcomed me back from a summer vacation in Europe.

By many definitions, it was the life we ALL dream of. For me, it was as amazing as I had dreamed it from the time I was five-years-old.

At that early age, I decided to become a millionaire when I grew up. My motivation was simple. I never wanted money to be a problem for me. I didn't want to financially struggle as was frequently the situation for my family. In fact, now, as I tell you my story, I can still remember the one day that changed my life. It was like it happened yesterday.

My family lived out in the country in the central part of Florida. It was a small village of only a few hundred people. Our home was a five-minute walk to a large lake which was my childhood playground. I built sand castles on the beach, swam, skied, and played on the docks. Our modest lifestyle was like many families in the area—people got by, but not much more.

The value of education was instilled in me by my mom, who was a school teacher. My father farmed and owned a citrus harvesting business. And my grandmother, my mom's mother, lived with us. She was an amazingly wise woman and a true angel who taught me the spiritual meaning of life. As I didn't have any brothers or sisters, she was part grandmother, sister, and close friend.

Dad had a strong entrepreneurial instinct in that he could easily spot trends and accurately predict where money could be made. However, he always seemed to have a setback at the very moment it looked like his financial life might turn around. He often had the right instincts, but his business endeavors never fully succeeded.

Dad was a man of strong character who cared deeply for others. He lived from his heart and believed in his fellow man. When Dad asked a customer how they felt or he expressed his concern over a problem, it came from his heart and they knew that he meant it. Relationships, both in his civic and business life, were his strong point.

With a magnetic personality, Dad was also a consummate storyteller. He was a true gentleman. Both men and women admired him and wanted to be around him. He was the type of man who instantly made friends wherever he traveled.

As a little boy I would go with him to the citrus groves, and we would fish together. I had boots that were just like Dad's, looked up to him, and wanted to emulate everything he did. Many of my life values were influenced by his. My desire to help others is the direct result of both my mom and dad's view that we all have an obligation to leave the world better off for our having journeyed here. This was like a family motto.

> At an early age, I decided to become a millionaire.

Now, it was probably just another typical day for my five-year-old friends, but not for me. I remember that day like it was just yesterday. I clearly recall the precise moment. I had such a strong awareness of what I wanted, like an epiphany, that it changed my life forever.

I ran into the house and looked up at my parents. Then I shouted out in my loudest little boy voice, "When I grow up, I'm going to be a millionaire!" Even now, I can remember the exact look of shock on Mom's face. She shook her finger at me and said in a hushed tone, "Don't tell anyone."

You see, we were good church-going people and my parents figured anyone who had that much money must be doing something wrong.

But like most little kids, I ignored what they said and told everyone in the neighborhood. It didn't matter to me what anyone else thought or if they even believed I could become a millionaire. What mattered is that I believed it.

I can even recall sketching out floor plans for mansions, though I'd never even been in one. From that day forward, I focused on my millionaire dream, determined that nothing would ever stop me or get in my way.

At five, I don't actually think I knew what a million dollars was; however, I figured if I had *that much money,* everything in my life would be great. I wouldn't have any problems! At least that is how I imagined my life as a millionaire.

Flash forward to age twenty-five, living in my new home on Bayshore Boulevard. Instead of a life of struggle, I now had money and an amazing lifestyle. For the first few months, I thought I had "arrived." This was everything I had dreamed of as a little boy. I even purchased the grand piano I had always wanted when I was taking piano lessons as a child.

But, you may be wondering how I arrived at this moment and place in my life. You are probably asking yourself how I made my first money and learned about business. Here is a brief version of the rest of my story.

I was in school in Los Angeles and had a month break. So, I flew back home to Florida to visit my parents. I had been away at college for several years and hadn't realized my father was facing mounting financial problems.

> We all have an obligation to leave the world better off for our having journeyed here.

After years of struggling in business, getting ahead multiple times only to have setbacks—freezes that wiped out crops, betrayals by business partners, unfortunate money decisions—Dad had reached the age of fifty-eight tired, worn-out, and feeling like a failure.

He had just sold one business to a competitor for pennies on the dollar. He needed to raise cash, but the money wasn't enough to pay off all his debts. Although he had recently negotiated a hauling contract that had excellent potential, his trucking lines were on the brink of financial bankruptcy. I was twenty-two years old at the time and had never seen my usually upbeat, optimistic father in a depressed mood.

Dad and I discussed his business situation numerous times during that month. He asked me to come home when I finished school, which was just months away, and help him with his businesses. This wasn't the future I'd imagined for myself.

Because of my family's rocky financial history, I had come to associate business with financial struggle. Therefore, I had carefully chosen to not take any business classes at college. In fact, I'd never read a business book or article. However, I agreed to help Dad short term, and at the age of twenty-three, I took over the general management of the family trucking lines. While I focused on management, Dad focused on the marketing and customer relationships.

What I quickly realized was that my father's caring heart and good nature, one that served him so well as a civic leader, actually made him an easy mark in the business world. This was only half the problem. Dad was also a shoot-from-the-hip, easy-going type of person. Unfortunately, his life philosophy was also his business philosophy.

I found there were no actual business plans or records; no policies, procedures or standards for employees or repairs; and worse, there was no formal billing system. Dad picked up the weekly checks from customers, but had no method to verify if they were accurate.

Adding to the calamity, I discovered there were financial liens that dated back for nine years. Dad was a good guy with good intentions. He simply didn't have the money to pay all the bills. I began to understand why Dad had frequently lost money, in spite of his keen eye for identifying where money could be made and his good nature that customers loved.

I began keeping notes throughout the day and studied them at night to determine what was working—and what wasn't. I made changes, often daily. As numbers were one of my strong points, I started keeping track of our loads hauled, issued weekly billing, and created a manual payroll system to pay the drivers.

I knew something was seriously wrong when we pulled hundreds of loads weekly, but could never keep any money in the bank. So, after about three months, I decided to spend a weekend pouring over the numbers and looking for a pattern.

In a flash it hit me! I immediately called Dad and said, "I've found the problem. Every week we take in less than we pay out. That's the reason we are constantly broke."

The rest of the weekend I thought about our situation and looked for a solution. Then it dawned on me. There was a shortage of trailers that could carry the type of cargo we hauled. That meant our customers needed us and would likely pay more for our services.

Monday morning I began calling customers and explained our rates were too low to stay in business. I was able to negotiate rate increases as large as twenty-five percent.

I then scheduled meetings with each of our suppliers and took new bids which lowered our prices. After discussing our maintenance problems with Dad, I took a bold move. We started our own maintenance company, leased a facility, hired two mechanics, and our repair costs quickly decreased. We were on a new path and I was ecstatic.

By the end of that first year, all the liens were paid off. We had progressed from large financial losses to a six figure profit. Within three years, we grew to six figure profits in a month. Over this time period, I hired a dispatcher, office manager and administrative team. We were growing and had become the #1 company in our niche.

I had an excitement that comes from making your first money and rewarded myself by purchasing the home on Bayshore Boulevard. However, that quickly wore off as the realization struck that my boyhood dream wasn't everything I had imagined it to be. I was making money but worked all the time and didn't even like what I was doing. I thought that becoming a millionaire would be the whole answer, but I wasn't happy nor was I fulfilled.

Rather than feeling like I was living in a utopia, my life increasingly felt more like a nightmare. I sought to wake up and *feel fully alive!* I wanted financial freedom. In fact I wanted to make additional millions, but I also needed freedom inside, the freedom that only comes from feeling inner peace and deep fulfillment.

For the next fifteen years, I embarked on a quest to find greater meaning by engaging in personal development courses and spiritual retreats. I explored paths to higher consciousness and delved deep within myself, searching for my purpose and why I was here on Earth.

During this time, I also pursued two more graduate degrees while continuing to run the trucking lines. I

> Rather than feeling like I was living in a utopia, my life increasingly felt more like a nightmare.

attended law school and obtained an MBA. Even with the new degrees and the financial freedom to travel, my life still lacked purpose. In my heart, I didn't feel that what I was doing really mattered.

I also hit a financial ceiling. Both the business growth and the profits stagnated. I no longer wanted to expand the companies. When new opportunities emerged, I actually found myself putting on the brakes instead of moving forward.

I had to find a resolution for the growing conflicts inside myself. My introspection brought me to realize that I was living my father's dream—at the cost of giving up my own. I grappled with this awareness and lost much sleep thinking about how to move forward.

I ultimately concluded that as deeply as I loved and was devoted to my Dad, *I had to leave and pursue my own path.* Having come to this decision point, I mounted an effort to sell the companies. As both my Dad and I had become equal partners, I had significant influence, but it took many discussions to bring him to an agreement to sell our business.

Although Dad was seventy-six and financially comfortable, Mom had died a few years earlier and he was afraid he wouldn't have anything important to do with his life. As he had always loved his civic work, I helped him develop a plan to become even more involved in his community.

Within three months of our selling the companies, Dad was the happiest I had seen him in years. He was giving back to others and beginning a new chapter of his life.

It was now time for me to pursue my own path. My quest launched me into long journeys, including a four-month, 30,000 mile road trip throughout Canada and the United States. I encountered a wide range of experiences as I traveled both in North America and around the world. At a Buddhist monastery I learned to meditate, and I participated in the work-study program at Esalen Institute—a human potential center on the Big Sur coast of California.

> I constantly sought to understand why I was here on Earth.

Throughout my journeys, I constantly sought to understand why I was here on Earth and how I could use my talents to make this a better world. Finally, on a day that was just as magical as that day I saw myself growing up to become a millionaire, my answer came to me. It filled my mind with a vision that I immediately knew was my calling.

For a couple of years I had been contemplating creating a millionaire program. However, I didn't want it to be another vapid, smoke-and-mirror, "get rich quick" show. I wanted to develop something that would have meaning and truly matter. I wanted it to create a lasting difference, both to the people whose lives I touch, and to the world.

And then, just like that, the answer revealed itself. I was relaxing in a spa tub, reading a brochure about an upcoming festival. Looking down, I read one word, *conscious*. The phrase immediately popped into my mind: "Conscious Millionaire®." I said it out loud and felt an instant experience of inner peace. I had found what I had been seeking. This profound awareness resonated throughout my being. I felt it to my core.

Over the next month I handled the legal matters, including incorporating the new business and filing trademarks. I developed my early business model and success plan. Then I scripted and recorded my first Conscious Millionaire audio program. This was the beginning of Conscious Millionaire Institute, LLC.

THE NEW ENTREPRENEUR PATH

There is a shift in consciousness that is occurring all over the globe. One of the ways it is most evident is in the rise of entrepreneurs who desire to achieve a higher purpose. These entrepreneurs want to make an important contribution both by how they live and how they conduct business. Just like you, they seek a path for consciously growing their business by making a difference.

The purpose of the Conscious Millionaire Institute is to provide you with the path, tools, and support needed to consciously grow your business.

Whether you are a seasoned entrepreneur or intend to start your first business, I acknowledge and commend you for seeking an entrepreneurial path that transcends the goal of only making money.

Entrepreneurs who choose this new path are driven to do something more with their lives.

First Stage Capitalism™, with its singular focus on creating profits, is giving way to a new approach that I call *Second Stage Capitalism*™. It is from this second stage that the new entrepreneur path emerges. Unlike its predecessor, this new approach has the dual focus of achieving both a higher purpose and higher profits. When entrepreneurs choose to build a business based on a heart desire to improve lives, organizations, and our world—both they and their team become driven by a shared desire to make a difference.

This more powerful, robust form of capitalism is fully expressed through *Conscious Millionaire*. It combines the drive to achieve something bigger with a focus on all the stakeholders winning together. As a result, it becomes a path for not only creating greater profits, but also achieving a greater good in the world.

This new path
combines profit with purpose.

Entrepreneurs who choose this new path are driven to do something more with their lives. Moreover, they take responsibility for their future by consciously choosing their destiny and taking focused action to attain it. This new Conscious Millionaire path takes business to a higher plane, a level of consciousness on which visionary purpose naturally emerges.

Reflect for a moment about your unmet dreams of touching and transforming others' lives. Consider the greatness you aspire to achieve and the mark you want to make on the world. Now imagine a path on which you can attain these goals by growing a business that helps others in ways that truly matter.

You also seek a path that supports your growing, learning, and expanding as a person. Like many other heart-felt people, you want to express your strongest passions in all you do, both in business and every area of your life. Equally important is your desire to experience deep fulfillment and abundant joy. You desire a path that not only provides you with each of these, but is also a way forward that supports your living with purpose.

You want to journey on a path that feels authentic and right. Moreover, you seek to experience a meaningful life that is lived in service of something greater than you. For many entrepreneurs who choose this new path, feeling a spiritual connection to a higher calling is important. It is how they unite their desire to serve mankind with their desire to serve a Higher Power.

This new path is as much about heart as it is about making money. It is a path on which your strongest passions, deepest sense of purpose, and greatest desire to make a difference in the world converge into one united path for consciously building your business.

This is the Conscious Millionaire Path, and it is with heartfelt appreciation that I thank you for choosing to journey with me through this book. I feel deeply honored. On this journey, I will help you define your visionary purpose, develop the skills you need, and learn to utilize the *Formula for Creating Wealth*™ so you can achieve whatever level of wealth you desire.

I Will Coach You

As you read *Conscious Millionaire,* I will be with you every step of the way to coach and guide you on your conscious path to millionaire wealth and success. My passion is helping entrepreneurs like you to achieve their true potential and consciously make their difference.

Your success is my personal interest and I look forward to hearing from you on our blog, membership site, and group coaching calls. I also look forward to meeting you in person at our live events. I want to know about your achievements and how you are utilizing the material in this book.

In every chapter, you will find several coaching tips to help you apply the material so you start experiencing fast results. Throughout the book you will find QR Codes and links that will take you to our membership site. As a special reader bonus, I am providing you with 30 days of *free access.*

Within the membership site, you will have access to bonus audio and video coaching segments as well as worksheets you can download. The bonus materials will help you increase your consciousness and grow your business in ways that add value to others and our society.

A coach helps you achieve
your results more quickly and easily.

As a business coach, I know how fast you can grow your business by using the formula, information, and tools you will find in this book.

Now, as a way for you to officially begin your millionaire journey, I invite you to set up your *Conscious Millionaire Journal.* Creating your journal is an important first step. It is a symbol both to yourself and me as your coach that you are committed to obtaining the most from this book.

If you didn't download your journal when you read the intro section "Get the Most from This Book," then go to our membership site and gain 30 days of *free access*; download your personal *Conscious Millionaire Journal.*

The journal contains valuable bonus material that will help you grow your business. If you don't have access to the Internet right now, you can still begin today by creating a handwritten journal on paper or in your word processor. Download your journal the next time you have Internet access so you have use of the *bonus* material in it.

Also, set up a new folder on your computer and name it "Conscious Millionaire." Save your journal in it, as well as any other downloads (as files) provided at the community membership site. That's it.

After you download your journal, open it and insert your name. Then either print it out so you can make manual entries or use the digital version on your computer or tablet.

Welcome to the Conscious Millionaire Community. I look forward to personally connecting with you as a new member. I invite you to read this book, whether a print copy or a digital e-book, with your journal open. Take notes and highlight the passages that speak to you. Open your mind and absorb this information. Make it a part of your consciousness.

> **Coaching:** Utilize the QR Code and link at the end of this chapter to sign-up for the Conscious Millionaire Membership site. As a reader, you receive 30 days of *free access*. Sign-up and download your *Conscious Millionaire Journal* now.

CLAIM YOUR FULL POWER

The exact moment you make a conscious decision to stop believing that life is happening to you and begin taking *conscious control* over your destiny, you start reclaiming your power. This is what it means to become conscious: it is assuming full responsibility for what you achieve and the fulfillment you have along your journey.

When you choose to believe and act like a victim, you feel powerless. What happens when you do this? You literally move the center of your power outside of yourself. It is as if your power has left your body and as a result, you may feel weak, stressed, or overloaded. You feel little to no commitment to your goals and have a hard time believing in yourself.

The instant you own your power, you begin to feel your power move back inside of you, into the center of your body. You become empowered. As this occurs, a renewed energy and passion fills you with new possibilities for your life and business. You feel powerful and become more committed to achieving at your highest level.

People who achieve millionaire wealth and fulfillment let go of anything that has held them back in their past. They choose to become aware of any internal roadblocks, make a conscious decision to move past them, and then focus on taking the actions that will create the results they want.

They claim their power, move through any fear, and hold themselves accountable for what they accomplish in their business and life. As a result, they experience significantly higher levels of wealth and success.

> **Coaching:** Choose something you want to achieve in your business but you are afraid you can't. Claim your power by choosing an initial action. Take it. Feel your power. Focus and take another action. Feel your power again. With each action you take, the more power you own.

Your Ideal Life and Business

Many entrepreneurs are so busy running their businesses that they never allow time to actually define what they most want, in their lives and their businesses. That is why I chose to include this section in the initial chapter of the book. In order for you to create your ideal life and business, including positioning yourself to only do what you truly enjoy, first define your ideal future.

Like most entrepreneurs, your ideal life includes much more than owning a business and making money. You probably also desire to enjoy the fulfillment that comes from sharing time with those you love and care about deeply. Further, a quality life includes engaging in activities that encourage you to grow, become healthy, and do something you feel matters.

Money only pays for your journey,
it's how you live your journey that matters!

What is the real secret to creating your ideal life and business? Design your business so that it fits into your life—rather than trying to fit your life into your business. Quite frankly, most entrepreneurs get this backwards. The only way to avoid this trap is to consciously design your ideal life first. Then create your business model and position so they complement the life you truly desire.

The time to begin doing this is today.

To receive the maximum value, ask any business partners to also complete this exercise. It is important to discover if each of your views of the future are complimentary, different, or currently incompatible. The reason is clear, isn't it? If there are any major incompatibilities in your respective views of the future, the best time to reconcile them is now.

In addition, if you have a significant other, also ask them to write their vision for each area. As life partners, it is important that you work together to design your shared, ideal future.

As you prepare to describe your ideal life, business, and position, I am going to invite you to dream big. Imagine that everything has gone according to your plan. In fact, it has actually turned out even *better*. Envision

Expand your mind to believe anything is possible.

the difference you want to make, the lives you want to touch, and the business you have enjoyed growing.

Expand your mind to believe anything is possible. As you consider the following questions create a vision of what you desire over the next three years:

1. Ideal Life: Describe your ideal Conscious Millionaire life. Describe a day in your life and what you do as you move through it. Where do you live and what is your dream lifestyle? Include the people in your life and the activities you enjoy sharing. What interests do you have in common? Describe your dream car, home, and personal items such as jewelry and things you collect. How does technology touch your life? Do you enjoy traveling and exploring the world? Do you like to be in nature? What sports, entertainment, and vacations do you want to experience?

Now, describe the characteristics of your closest friends. Envision the type of activities that you enjoy doing with them. Name any people you admire. Would you like to meet them? Imagine your ideal romantic relationship. If you have someone you care about, describe what most attracts you to them. Consider what it means for you to live consciously. How does this influence the choices you make about your health, your food choices, how you interact with our environment—your total lifestyle? To live consciously, make choices that feel authentic and right for you.

Notice how you see yourself helping others and giving back. Does your life include supporting specific causes? Will you begin your own non-profit? How will life on our planet be different because you journeyed here?

Coaching: Open your *Conscious Millionaire Journal* you downloaded from the membership site. Write a description of what your ideal life looks and feels like in three years.

2. Ideal Business: Describe the type of business you envision owning in three years. If you currently own a business, notice what may have changed, such as the range of products and services you sell, how you market, and the size of your revenues and profits. What is the over arching purpose or vision for your business? Why does it inspire you? What would be missing in your customers' lives if your business didn't exist?

How large has your customer base grown in three years? In what new ways are you engaging with your community? Consider what you most enjoy about your business, your office environment, and the people with whom you work. Describe the characteristics of your office, including whether it is inside or outside your home. Is your ideal business people-driven or would you automate most activities and have few employees?

Describe the major challenges and opportunities you envision for your business three years from now. *For example*: how to manage growth, develop a sales team, or oversee virtual contractors located throughout the world. How fast are you growing and what are your best avenues for growth? Are there multiple locations? Have you franchised? How will you leverage your business? Describe your coaches, mentors, advisory team and key team members.

> **Coaching:** Open your *Conscious Millionaire Journal*. Write a description of what your ideal business looks and feels like in three years. Include the major difference your business will make, how it will help others.

3. Ideal Position: Imagine your primary role in your business in three years. Begin creating the position you want by imagining what you would be doing on your ideal day. Walk through it in your mind. What would occur? Are you only performing activities that are your strengths and passions? Have you delegated or out-sourced everything you dislike or are not good at? Remember, you are designing your ideal position.

Make certain that it is 100 percent the way you want it. Next, consider your leadership style. Will you create the rules in a top down fashion or operate collaboratively? What fits your personality? Think about what you see yourself doing. Then review the following list and consider which you want to include in your position: networking, leading your team, developing new products, speaking, media interviews, marketing, sales, or negotiating deals.

In your ideal position, will you work in a physical office or virtually, from anywhere in the world? How often would you travel on business and how much time would you take off from work? How many hours would you work each week? Create your ideal position, the one that will allow you to contribute to your business, clients, and the world at your highest levels.

Coaching: Open your *Conscious Millionaire Journal* Write a description of what your ideal position looks and feels like in three years.

CONSCIOUS MILLIONAIRE COACHING

Build Your Strategy

Open your *Conscious Millionaire Journal*. Write a three-step business strategy using *conscious focused action*. Develop your strategy utilizing the concept provided in the *conscious* step below. It is an important concept from this chapter.

1. Conscious: Define the characteristics of other entrepreneurs with whom you want to build a relationship. Utilize these characteristics to create a goal. *For example:* If you want to build a group of friends and associates who also seek to become millionaires, your goal could be, "Develop one new relationship each month with an entrepreneur who is committed to becoming a Conscious Millionaire."

2. Focused: As you focus on your goal, choose three actions that will help you begin to achieve it. Determine the precise order for your actions.

3. Action: During the next twenty-four hours, execute by taking your three actions.

Grow Your Business

In your *Conscious Millionaire Journal* make notes on how you utilize each of the following to grow your business:

• Select an aspect of the "New Entrepreneur Path" with which you strongly identify. How will you utilize it to grow your business?

• Use the *ideal business* description you developed in the prior section and choose three actions you can take this week to create your ideal business.

continued

- Utilize the *ideal position* description you developed in the prior section and choose three actions you can take this week to begin creating it.

Create your journey

Becoming a Conscious Millionaire involves making conscious choices. In each chapter you will find three suggested choices for what to read next. The first is to read another *conscious* section. The second is to read another *millionaire* section. The third choice is to *journey* through the book linearly, reading it chapter by chapter.

Conscious: Consider reading the "Purpose Gives You Direction" section in Chapter 4, *Passion, Purpose, and Values*, before continuing to the next chapter.

Millionaire: Take a look at "How to Achieve Big Goals" section in Chapter 14, *Create Your Millionaire Plan*, before going to the next chapter.

Journey: Continue forward to Chapter 2, *Formula for Creating Wealth*.

QR Code / Link

Go to the Conscious Millionaire membership site and sign up for your Free membership now. Then download your *Conscious Millionaire Journal*. You will want to utilize it to complete your coaching exercises in this book. Access the site now at:
ConsciousMillionaire.com/member

Use this QR Code / link to sign up for the next *Mindset to Make Millions* program. Regularly $97, this is a FREE Reader Bonus. In it you will discover how to consciously create wealth and enjoy a life of total abundance. Sign-up at:
ConsciousMillionaire.com/mindset

CHAPTER 2

FORMULA FOR CREATING WEALTH

*Action only matters when it is
consciously focused on your goals.*

In this chapter, you discover the power of making choices consciously. You will learn the three-part *Formula for Creating Wealth*, which is based on becoming conscious, being focused, and taking action. You will then be introduced to the foundational version of the *Conscious Focused Action Model*™. This model applies the formula to help you achieve any result you desire. You will also discover how to achieve your results quickly by accessing the amazing power of *Conscious Millionaire Visualization*™.

THE POWER OF CONSCIOUS CHOICE

Throughout your day, you make numerous choices in your business and in your life. At the conscious level, you make hundreds, if not thousands, of choices every day. At the unconscious level, you make an incalculable number of choices daily, as well. Whether small or massively significant, every choice is a decision that affects the results you achieve.

Choices are statements about your priorities and what you value. They are decisions about your desires and how you will achieve them. Each choice you make both opens and closes doors. Doors open by providing access to specific opportunities. Doors close by eliminating any other options.

> Your choices determine whether you operate from higher consciousness or remain unconscious of the consequences.

Consider all of the choices you make in your business. You choose the type of business you own, your vision and values for it, the customers you serve, the people on your team, the products and services you provide, and the prices at which they're offered.

You choose whether to structure your daily activities and consciously choose priorities, or haphazardly go through your day, hoping something good will happen. You also choose whether to stay laser focused, or allow yourself to become distracted and veer off course. You choose how you respond to everything that occurs throughout your day.

You determine how rapidly your business grows, which goals you will pursue, as well as the actions you choose to take. You select which opportunities to follow and how well you manage each of the risks involved. You choose the level of difference you make in our world.

Whether you build a culture that attracts the top talent and then fosters their growth is also your choice. You choose whether your business is only focused on profits or is also designed to achieve a larger purpose and provide fulfillment to all those involved, such as your team, suppliers, and customers.

While many people may argue with the following statement, until you accept the truth in it, I guarantee that you will have far less money and success than I believe you deserve: The level of financial success you currently have is the direct result of *your choices*.

Simply put, your choices determine whether you operate from higher consciousness or remain unconscious of the consequences—for yourself, others, and our world. Your choices also determine whether you build a high growth, profitable business or constantly lose money, and whether you improve the lives of your customers or sell products that deliver little value.

The reality is you are constantly making choices. Your business and personal life demands this of you. However, the problem is most entrepreneurs don't *consciously* consider all of their options before choosing which actions to take.

> The level of financial success you currently have is the direct result of *your choices*.

They jump into the middle of building their business without setting up the first part, which is getting clear about the results they want to achieve. Until you develop clear goals, you can't choose the best actions to take. Furthermore, you can't develop the best business model or success plan. Your first step must be to consciously choose what you want.

Entrepreneurs who achieve the most,
take responsibility by making conscious choices!

The entrepreneurs who make the biggest differences, grow the biggest businesses, and enjoy amazing lives that are deeply fulfilling, all take personal responsibility for achieving what they desire. They realize that the only way to control their future is to assume responsibility by making conscious choices. If you want to take control over your financial future, then consciously choose your destiny and take *conscious focused actions* to attain it.

Coaching: Open your *Conscious Millionaire Journal*. In it describe a business choice you will make this week. Consider at least three options and list the positive and negative consequences of choosing each of these. Then consciously choose one option and put it into action.

The Formula For Creating Wealth

Success is not an accident. Entrepreneurs who achieve greatness all follow a consistent method. In short, they achieve their financial results because they use a specific formula. So, what is a formula? It is a process, a set of steps that you can use to obtain predictable results in your business, finances, and life. It is a repeatable way to achieve results.

In this section you discover what I believe is the *ultimate* formula for achieving wealth. This formula consists of three specific steps. Even before I fully articulated them, I was utilizing them to create wealth from my businesses.

The Formula for Creating Wealth
empowers you to achieve any result you desire!

These steps, which I now call the *Formula for Creating Wealth*, are what allowed me to progress from growing up in a family that frequently struggled financially to becoming a millionaire in my twenties. Consistently applying these three steps is the reason I could afford to live in a luxury town home on the water, enjoy my dream car, and vacation in Europe, at the age of twenty-five.

It is also how I reached every major goal I've ever accomplished. This includes how I am building the non-profit I founded,

Conscious World® Foundation, Inc. You can utilize this formula to achieve any result you desire—in your business and life.

When I sat down to write *Conscious Millionaire,* the first question I asked was, "How did I create wealth so quickly?" That's when I realized there were three steps I had been taking all along. These aren't just the steps for achieving financial wealth; they are also the steps for attaining any type of professional or personal success you desire.

The *Formula for Creating Wealth* is: *conscious focused action*™. Think of these three steps as the skills to develop and master if you want to consciously create wealth.

The following model provides a visual representation of the formula. The first level is *conscious*; at this level become conscious of the specific result you desire. The second level is *focus*; at this level focus on your desired result so you stay on track to achieve it. The third level is *action*; at this level take actions focused on assuring you attain your result.

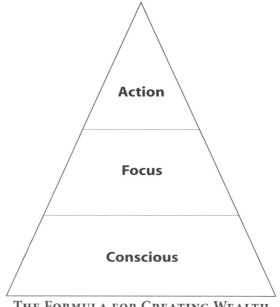

THE FORMULA FOR CREATING WEALTH

1. Conscious: To become conscious is to awaken. It is to become aware of who you are, which includes your deeper passions, sense of purpose and greatest strengths. It is to become aware of both your interior and exterior worlds. It is also to realize that you are part of a greater whole, one that includes you, others, and the society in which you live.

To be conscious as an entrepreneur means giving attention to the mechanics of making money, including: how to define your ideal customer, choose the right products, market and sell them, and create profitable growth. Being conscious includes gathering information, then analyzing it before you make decisions or choose a course of action. As a business leader and entrepreneur it means realizing that you have a responsibility not only to yourself, but to others and the world in which you live.

When you make financial and business decisions, it is noticing which decisions have integrity and genuinely improve the lives of others, and which do not, then only taking actions that feel authentic and right for you. By paying attention to what is in your heart—the authentic ways you want to help others, then expressing these in your business purpose—you will not only make a powerful difference, you will create your highest profits.

The reason is simple. When you and your team are achieving something that matters to each of you, a purpose that transcends money itself, you will become passionately motivated to achieve it. Because you are motivated, you will grow your business faster.

As you become more conscious, you become more aware of your innate potential, increase your desire to learn and grow, and expand your views of what is possible. As you develop your awareness, you increase your ability to connect with higher levels of consciousness—states in which bigger visions are born. As you take your conscious journey, you will discover an infinite number of opportunities to create wealth.

On this journey, you will discover there are three types of consciousness: *awareness, visionary,* and *social.* Awareness consciousness is knowing what you want, how to best achieve it, and what is true in the present moment. Visionary consciousness relates to connecting to a higher consciousness, which is a source of inspiration and vision. Social consciousness is being mindful of the needs of others and the problems in society, then responding to these in how you build your business and live your life.

Conscious Millionaires operate with a sense of higher consciousness. They build their businesses with the complimentary goals of achieving a higher purpose and making higher profits.

2. Focused: To become focused is to concentrate your attention in a specific direction. Focus is the ability to follow one course of action to completion rather than succumbing to distractions. When you scatter your focus, your energy dissipates over a broad spectrum. As a result, you accomplish very little and your business tends to stagnate. Yet, when you become laser focused, you naturally build momentum and achieve your goals faster. The more you focus your attention in a specific direction, the more your entire business begins to move in that direction.

By paying attention to the feedback you receive, you become aware of which *conscious focused actions* to take.

If you focus on bringing your visionary purpose into your business, you identify ways to infuse it into every area of your business. If you focus on increasing profits, you find ways to ramp up profits. By focusing on building products that deliver high value, you will naturally discover ways to develop it. If you focus on acquiring customers and making more sales, you begin to attract customers and make more sales.

While every entrepreneur has the same number of minutes, hours, and days in a week, the ones who become successful, consciously focus on their highest *priorities* and best use of their time. As a result, they achieve far more than other entrepreneurs because they execute by taking the most effective and efficient actions.

3. Action: One of the primary differences between the big winners in business and those who perform poorly is execution. Successful entrepreneurs constantly take action; but not just any action. In fact, one of the most frequent errors business owners make is jumping right in and taking massive action—without allowing time to reflect consciously on what they want and how they can best achieve it.

However, entrepreneurs who utilize the *Formula for Creating Wealth* become *conscious* of the specific results they want, are laser *focused* on achieving them, and efficiently reach their results by taking *actions* only designed to attain them.

The most successful entrepreneurs don't just take the right actions, they take them quickly. They are the *first* to create upgraded products, deliver innovative services, or implement cutting-edge marketing strategies. Conscious Millionaire entrepreneurs achieve higher results by remaining consciously focused on their desired results, then taking the *fewest* number of actions necessary to achieve their results.

This is an iterative formula, which means you go through the three levels numerous times. Each time make changes. This allows you to learn more about what works and what doesn't at every level. By paying attention to the feedback you receive, you become aware of which *conscious focused actions* to take.

Consciousness makes you aware of the result you want and the strategies that will help you achieve it. Focus drives your energy in the direction of that result. Action moves you forward toward your desired result. In the next section, you will learn how to use the formula to grow your business, create wealth, and achieve any business result you desire.

Coaching: Open your *Conscious Millionaire Journal*. Describe one goal that will require you to move outside your current comfort zone. Then take the first three actions necessary to achieve it as a way to expand your consciousness of what is possible for you.

Conscious Focused Action Model

The model consists of five levels: *conscious*, *focus*, *action*, *result*, and *learning*. The first three levels come from *The Formula for Creating Wealth*, which was introduced in the prior section.

The *Conscious Focused Action Model* adds a fourth and fifth level. The fourth level, *result*, is the specific result you chose when at the conscious level. The fifth level, *learning*, is the highest level of the model. It is at this level that you discover what worked and what didn't.

Then based upon what you learn, make decisions about what needs to change and iterate. What this means is return to the conscious level, introduce the needed changes into the model, then move through the five levels of the model again.

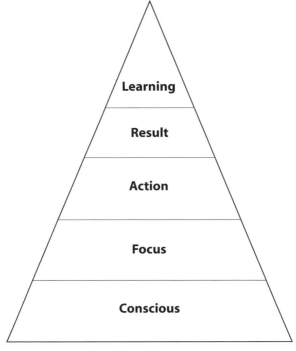

The Five Levels

Now that you have been introduced to the five levels that comprise the *Conscious Focused Action Model*, in this section you will learn how to use the three focal points on each of the five levels.

Because the following description contains many details, I suggest you use the QR Code and link at the end of this chapter to access a coaching video which fully explains the first diagram, which is below. The short video will give you a practical example of how to use each of the levels.

Throughout *Conscious Millionaire,* there are fourteen versions of this model. Chapters two through fourteen contain one or more of these versions. Each version helps you apply the information in the chapter to become a Conscious Millionaire. Think of these models as your guide for creating wealth.

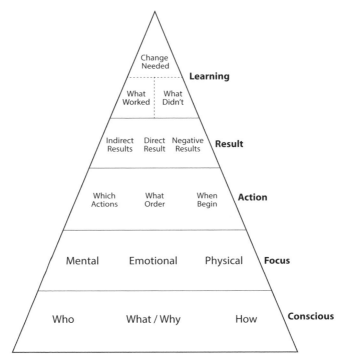

CONSCIOUS FOCUSED ACTION MODEL-1

Let's use your desire to become a Conscious Millionaire as an example for how to use the Model.

1. Conscious Level

At the conscious level, address these three areas:

A. "**What** result do I want to achieve?" and, "**Why** is accomplishing this result a priority?" These questions address which *result* you desire (to become a Conscious Millionaire) and why it is a priority for you.

B. "**Who** will benefit from achieving this result?" In this example, it is you. Note: it could also be others or society. In addition consider, "**Who** will help attain this result?"

C. "**How** do I best reach this result?" which brings you to consider: skills, strategy (set of actions) and resources (people, assets, money).

2. Focus Level

At the focus level, develop these three focal points:

A. **Mental** (thoughts, beliefs, questions)

B. **Emotional** (positive emotions)

C. **Physical** (readiness to take action)

Develop mental focus by constantly thinking about how to achieve your direct result; creating empowering beliefs that support you achieving that result; and, asking yourself questions that direct your mind to discover solutions for how to best achieve your result. Develop emotional focus by selecting three to five positive emotions that you can utilize as positive states. Develop physical focus by maintaining your health and being constantly focused on taking action.

3. Action Level

At the action level, consider these three questions:

A. "Which actions should I take?"

B. "What order should I take them?"

C. "When should I begin taking action?"

While answering these questions, identify any internal and external events that must occur before you begin to take action. Internal events could include other team members completing their part of a project. External events might include when a prospect indicates interest in buying.

4. Result Level

At the result level, think of three aspects of your results:

A. Direct result: how well you achieved the result you intended;

B. Indirect results: other positive outcomes that weren't your specific focus (such as your customer referring a friend); and

C. Negative results: negative outcomes that hinder achieving your desired outcome (such as spending so much time working that you become sick, which costs several days of productivity).

5. Learning Level

At the learning level, evaluate your experience by asking:

A. "What worked?"

B. "What didn't work?"

C. "What change is needed?"

If you didn't fully achieve your desired result, want to improve your process, or care to achieve your result at a higher level, then iterate. Here is how to iterate: determine what needs to change, return to the conscious level, then make the changes as you move through the model again.

To identify any needed changes, review the decisions you made at each level and consider alternatives that might be better. Make these changes and *test them* to see if they actually are better. How? Put them in the model and notice your results.

By continuing to iterate, you will develop your ideal process (your best *conscious focused actions*) for achieving your specific result. Once you develop your ideal process, you can easily teach it to new employees and duplicate it at other locations. You can also sell it to other entrepreneurs as an information product, consulting service or as part of franchising your business.

While our example concerns a result you want to achieve for yourself, the model can also be utilized to provide a benefit to others (such as another person, business, organization) or to society. Many people find the best way to think of society is as a community to which you belong or care about. Recall that at the *conscious* level of the model, the three possibilities for "who" will benefit are: you, others and society/community.

By utilizing this five-level model in any of the fourteen variations you will find throughout Conscious Millionaire, you can rapidly grow your business and achieve any result you desire.

Coaching: Open your *Conscious Millionaire Journal.* Write one result you want to achieve in your business. Then utilize the five levels of the *Conscious Focused Action* Model to achieve it.

Conscious Millionaire Visualization

Visualizing is thinking in terms of pictures. Think of a gold coin or blue sky and you are visualizing. Successful athletes, actors, speakers, singers, entrepreneurs, business owners, sales professionals and executives all use some form of visualization to turn their goals into real life results. High performers regularly visualize their success before it happens.

Olympic athletes and major sports players use visualization to help them win and stay at the top of their game. They envisage hitting their golf shot, winning their race, making the touchdown, sinking the ball, and making the goal. Just as they use visualization to see themselves winning before the game begins, you can use visualization to see yourself winning in your business.

Remember when you were a child? You would imagine whatever you desired. You easily accessed your imagination and saw yourself becoming rich and famous, being a movie star, a celebrity singer with raving fans, living in an amazing home, driving your ideal car, or having your dream boyfriend or girlfriend.

In your mind, you visited imaginary lands and became a pretend person. You would see yourself taking action in such rich and vivid detail that you completely felt and believed it was real. You experienced the emotional excitement as if you had actually become a king, queen or action hero.

What were you doing? You were visualizing. As an entrepreneur, you can now use those same powers to help rapidly turn your goals into the results you want. You can use visualization to help grow your business, lead your team, close more sales, or achieve any result you desire.

> High performers regularly visualize their success before it happens.

Remember the childhood story I shared with you? I was a five-year-old when I saw myself growing up to become a millionaire. What was I doing? I was visualizing. I've been constantly refining my approach since. As a result, I've developed a massively powerful process that I am sharing with you now. Use it to achieve any business or personal goal you desire.

I call my approach *Conscious Millionaire Visualization*. It consists of three steps, each modeled after one of the steps in the *Formula for Creating Wealth*:

1. Conscious: In your mind, build a richly detailed, vivid picture of your ideal future, the new reality that you want to experience. Describe what you will specifically see, hear, smell, taste, physically sense and emotionally feel when what you desire has fully become your new reality. See it in your mind as it will be when your goal is fully achieved—see it as if your quest is finished.

2. Focused: Intensely focus your mind, heart-centered feelings and body on your desired reality. Imagine that every thought, feeling and cell in your body is laser focused on your outcome. Instead of leaving the picture "out there," as if it were somewhere in the distant future, bring it toward you. When it gets close to your body, bring it inside of you so your future and present become ONE. Embody it and see yourself fully living in your new reality, RIGHT NOW!

3. Action: While connecting with your passionate heart-centered feelings, mentally rehearse the exact step-by-step actions you believe are necessary in order to create your new reality. Continue to make any needed changes in your actions until you genuinely feel and totally believe that by taking these actions you will create your new reality. Think of this as your action script. While in a state of intense mental, emotional and physical focus, take your initial three action steps. Remain in your "visualization state" as you move forward through your day.

Conscious Millionaire Visualization is how I visualize and is what I teach my clients. By not only mentally taking ownership of what you want, but also emotionally feeling and physically sensing your desired reality, you can rapidly move toward the result you want. Start your day by visualizing your success and taking *conscious focused action* to make it your new reality.

One of the *secrets* to why *Conscious Millionaire Visualization* consistently produces amazing results is found in the "focused" step. When you fully associate in your mind, heart, and body with your desired result as being *completed*, you energetically become one with your desired result. At the exact moment this occurs, you experience a deep transformational shift—in your mind, emotions, and body.

The shift is from hoping the result will occur someday in the future, to experiencing it as if it is already occurring today—here and now, in this exact moment. This approach to visualization is a practical expression of a profound truth: all creation begins on the internal plane and manifests on the external plane—as within, so without. This truth is expressed in every culture and wisdom tradition known to mankind.

> Through this form of visualization, you give yourself permission to live at your highest level.

Using *Conscious Millionaire Visualization,* you create your reality. How? By visualizing with complete faith that what you are seeing in your mind, feeling in your heart, and sensing in your body is real—*as if* it is already occurring. Through this form of visualization, you give yourself permission to live at your highest level and express your highest consciousness.

Your *internal* reality is literally activated and magnified through the visualization process. It is made ready to manifest outside of you. Therefore, act with complete confidence, believing that what you are *seeing* in your mind, *feeling* in your heart, and *sensing* in your body is becoming your *external* reality—one *conscious focused action* at a time.

By utilizing *Conscious Millionaire Visualization*, you make it possible for your highest and best self, the expression of your deepest passions and greatest aspirations, to become your reality in this very moment. This is true whether it is achieving your purpose, closing a sale, growing your business, or attaining any goal that is important to you.

At the end of this chapter, there is a QR Code and link to a coaching audio on our membership site. It will help you develop the skill of *Conscious Millionaire Visualization*.

CONSCIOUS MILLIONAIRE COACHING

Build Your Strategy

Open your *Conscious Millionaire Journal.* Write a three-step business strategy using *conscious focused action.* Develop your strategy utilizing the concept provided in the *conscious* step below. It is an important concept from this chapter.

1. Conscious: Develop a goal to increase your profits. *For example*: "Choose the goal of growing your profits by 10% each month compared to the prior month. Continue this goal each month for the next twelve months."

2. Focused: As you focus on your goal, choose three actions that will help you begin to achieve it. Determine the precise order for your actions.

3. Action: During the next twenty-four hours, execute by taking your three actions.

Grow Your Business

In your *Conscious Millionaire Journal* make notes on how you utilize each of the following to grow your business:

• Consciously select a financial result you want to achieve in your business; then develop a list of actions you could take to achieve it.

• Utilizing the result you chose above, develop a list of three positive beliefs (mental focus) that would help you attain it.

• Use Conscious Millionaire Visualization to focus on the financial result you chose above. This week, spend five minutes each morning visualizing yourself achieving it. Notice that when you visualize, *you feel the result is already occurring,* which makes it easier for you to take *conscious focused actions* to attain it.

continued

Create Your Journey

Becoming a Conscious Millionaire involves making conscious choices. In each chapter, you will find three suggested choices for what to read next. The first is to read another *conscious* section. The second is to read another *millionaire* section. The third choice is to *journey* through the book linearly, reading it chapter by chapter.

 Conscious: Consider reading the "From Scarcity to Abundance" section in Chapter 8, *Create an Abundance Mindset*, before continuing to the next chapter.

 Millionaire: Take a look at the "Leverage Your Business Relationships" section in Chapter 10, *Build Powerful Relationships*, before going to next chapter.

 Journey: Continue forward to Chapter 3, *Win by Becoming Conscious*.

QR Codes / Links

 View a coaching video that explains *The Formula For Creating Wealth*. Access the site now at: **ConsciousMillionaire.com/member**

 View a coaching video that reveals how to best utilize the *Conscious Focused Action Model*. Access the site now at: **ConsciousMillionaire.com/member**

 Listen to a coaching audio that guides you through *Conscious Millionaire Visualization*. Access the site now at: **ConsciousMillionaire.com/member**

CHAPTER 3

WIN BY BECOMING CONSCIOUS

Success begins with awareness.

In this chapter, you learn how biology, physics, psychology, and an understanding of consciousness come together to create the new *Science of Conscious Success*™. You will also discover the three types of consciousness and consider your conscious calling. Further, you will learn how to expand your consciousness by viewing life through three lenses: yourself, others, and society. You will be introduced to the *New Wealth Consciousness*™ and the nine beliefs that define it. You will also utilize the *Conscious Focused Action Model* to move forward on your Conscious Millionaire Journey.

SCIENCE OF CONSCIOUS SUCCESS

We are living in the most exciting moment in history. Our evolution as a species and the evolution in our sciences are coming together. We now understand how to utilize the human potential at a higher level than ever before. By combining discoveries in biology, physics, psychology, and consciousness, I developed a new science—the *Science of Conscious Success*.

Biology was the first area in which we began to understand how we can consciously choose our destiny rather than being controlled by beliefs and ways of viewing ourselves which we learned earlier in life. How we make this change is found in the way our brains operate.

Through the process of evolution, we developed the frontal lobe. This provides us with the capacity for self-reflection. It provides us with a way to connect with higher consciousness and develop meaningful interpretations of life.

Because of your ability to self-reflect, you can consciously choose the results you *focus* on and which *actions* you take. As a result, you can now break free from old habits, and consciously take charge of your destiny. Not just as individuals, but as a society we are consciously evolving. We are developing more conscious ways of doing business, handling environmental and social issues, and interacting with one another. We are taping into new dimensions of what's possible.

> We are living in the most exciting moment in history.

Each of us also has the ability to bring unconscious material, such as hidden beliefs, emotions, or internal road blocks, into your consciousness. Once you are aware of them, you can *consciously* choose to change them. This provides you with the ability to update your beliefs by transforming old beliefs into ones that support you.

It is your *conscious capacity* that empowers you to expand what you see as possible, conceive of bigger visions, and achieve bigger differences. Hence, you can add more value, grow your business faster, and create a greater legacy.

Physics has also created breakthroughs that contribute to this new *Science of Conscious Success*. In the early 1900s, Einstein discovered that everything is energy. This includes both the physical material you see and everything you don't see, such as your thoughts and emotions.

Einstein put this into his now famous formula, $E = MC^2$. However, you don't need to know anything about science to understand that we live in an energy universe.

Think about the people, activities, and foods you enjoy that give you energy. Now think about people, activities, and foods that pull your energy down. Notice how positive and negative experiences affect your energy differently.

Physicists discovered that energy is attracted to other energy which is vibrating at the same frequency. You've probably experienced this with a close friend or partner. When you feel in sync with them, it's as if you are both thinking the same thoughts. You can often finish one another's sentences. It's like you are on the same frequency. And you are.

This includes the group consciousness that emerges when you are at an event, a concert or conference. You have probably had the experience of being in a group where all the people around you seemed to share the same thoughts and emotions. This is what it means to experience group consciousness.

Create an inner thought, feeling,
and cellular vibration of abundant wealth.

Being attracted to energy that is vibrating at your frequency is called the *law of attraction*. What this means is very simple. If you want to attract million dollar opportunities and create high levels of financial wealth, then first change your energy so it matches the vibrations of what you desire. Simply put, wealth manifests from the inside out.

Therefore if you want to become wealthy, then first develop thoughts, feelings, and a consciousness of wealth. The same is true for anything else you want to create through your business or your life.

For example: Use the *Conscious Millionaire Visualization* to shift your energy to match the level of wealth you want. As you do, you will both attract and become attracted to anything that will help you achieve the specific level of wealth you desire.

This leads us to psychology, which is the third area in the *Science of Conscious Success*. Psychology helps you change your beliefs, mindset, and emotions.

Psychology began as a science in the late 1800s. The breakthroughs in this area help us to both achieve at our highest level and become more fulfilled in the process. Important discoveries in psychology include how the conscious and unconscious aspects of your mind operate. They also include how to manage your mental and emotional state, achieve high performance, and create rapid belief shifts using *Energy Psychology*.

Because of these changes, we now have amazing tools and technologies that help us unlock our inner potential. You can use these to remove internal roadblocks, such as negative emotions, fears, and energy blocks. You can also use them to create rapid changes in your beliefs and mindset.

> The *Science of Conscious Success* empowers you to unlock your potential, choose your destiny, and attain it.

At college, I originally studied pre-medicine, which included biology and physics. Then I received a Masters in Psychology, my first graduate degree. This was followed by nine years of training and certifications in NLP® (Neuro-Linguistic Programming), Ericksonian Hypnosis®, and Psych-K®, which is part of the new energy psychology. I also learned to meditate at a Buddhist Monastery and have studied extensively both western and eastern approaches to consciousness and awareness. In addition to these studies, I developed my analytical skills by acquiring both a law degree and MBA.

It is because of my background in these areas that I was able to create the *Science of Conscious Success.* In addition to the above discussion, this new science also provides an understanding of how to do the following:

- learn faster and easier

- make conscious choices

- utilize your whole brain

- create your results faster

- eliminate your old beliefs

- achieve your highest potential

- connect with higher consciousness

The *Science of Conscious Success* empowers you to unlock your potential, choose your destiny, and attain it.

Types of Consciousness

There are three types of consciousness: *Awareness* Consciousness helps you awaken to what is true now, what changes you want to make, and how best to achieve them. *Visionary* Consciousness allows you to tap into higher states of consciousness and become aware of expanded possibilities; this includes ways you can innovate and develop new products. *Social* Consciousness helps you understand the needs of other people and our society. This includes both the communities and environment in which we live and work.

Cultivating each of these empowers you to make a greater difference and achieve greater wealth. Here is an overview of each dimension:

1. Awareness Consciousness: This is the type of consciousness that relates to making conscious choices rather than just reacting without reflection. The truth is everything in your business and personal life is an expression of your current level of awareness. The best way to take control over your financial destiny is to become aware of what you want, then identify the best options for achieving it. When you become aware, you wake up and notice what is true about:

• **Your business:** and the top priorities you need to address at this time;

• **Your customers:** and how you can best solve their problems and better serve them; and,

• **Our world:** and how you can be of greater service as well as how to create wealth by becoming conscious of major trends.

To attain wealth consciously, become aware of the very mechanics of making money; which goals and strategies are right for your business; and how to unlock your potential to become a high performer.

2. Visionary Consciousness: This type of consciousness relates to connecting with a higher level of inspiration, which is also called "Higher Consciousness." In various spiritual disciplines, this is viewed as moving from "small mind," which is your personal mind, into "big mind," which is the larger mind of the universe. When you tap into visionary consciousness, you enter into a higher state of consciousness and access a level of information that inspires greater innovation for life, business, and society.

Many entrepreneurs, business owners, and leaders as well as writers, artists, and inventors, regularly connect with this dimension of consciousness. In this state of consciousness, they look at the future differently. They both envision and develop innovative ideas, products, and services. These innovations improve the quality of customers' lives; how organizations operate; the way society solves problems; and how people live, work, and play.

As a personal example, I wrote much of *Conscious Millionaire* by connecting with visionary consciousness.

3. Social Consciousness: This type of consciousness refers to being mindful, or concerned in a caring and compassionate way, about how your actions affect the whole of humanity. Because of our understanding of quantum physics, we now realize that you and I are part of an interconnected whole, a seamless web of life. This web is an energy field that connects each of us with everything on this planet. Because we are all interconnected, there is no such thing as a small action. At some level, each of our actions affects the whole of humanity.

> Social entrepreneurs seek to make a difference that is measured in a positive return to society.

In response to the increase in social consciousness, a new, socially aware entrepreneur has emerged. These new social entrepreneurs combine a profit motive with solving social issues. They build businesses that focus on areas such as: reducing pollution, providing clean drinking water, promoting the economic well-being of impoverished people, feeding and housing the world's growing population, and promoting healthier lifestyles.

This new social entrepreneur utilizes entrepreneurial principles to create a venture designed to achieve social change. For many social entrepreneurs, it is social change, rather than profit, that is the primary goal and motivator. Social entrepreneurs seek to make a difference that is measured in a positive return to society.

Coaching: Open your *Conscious Millionaire Journal*. Describe one product or service concept that would both help your customer and benefit society. *For example*: A product could be a toxic-free house cleaner that would both improve the health of your customer and create a better environment; a service could be roofing that both saves customers money and lasts longer.

Your Conscious Calling

My parents taught me that we are all on Earth to make a difference. When we leave, the world should be better off because we journeyed here. I was brought up to believe that living a good life includes helping others and making my personal difference. This is the reason I established the Conscious Millionaire Institute. I want to support entrepreneurs in both discovering the difference they desire to make and creating their livelihood by expressing it to the world.

I believe we each have a calling, a reason we are here. For some there is a spiritual dimension to their calling. For others, the experience is more of a profound awareness they are here to achieve something important—something that matters.

You are on earth to
make an important difference!

Your calling grabs you at the deepest levels of who you are. It tugs at your heart strings and resonates with your soul. It expands your consciousness and awakens you to your true potential of what is possible for your life.

Wherever you are on your journey of discovering your personal calling, in this book you will find the tools you need to *define the difference* you want to make; then turn it into a *way to make money.*

Every person who makes a *big* difference begins with a *big* vision of how life can become better. His or her desire is to help individuals, organizations, or society improve in some way. People who *consciously* create a big vision, then focus on putting it into action, are the true visionaries of any period.

You are one of those people. That is why you were attracted to *Conscious Millionaire.* It is why you have an inner drive to create a difference with your life.

The truth is we all dream of how things could be different. Every time you visualize your life or the world being different, you are dreaming of a better future. That dream is your vision of what is possible.

> People who consciously create a big vision, then focus on putting it into action, are the true visionaries.

People who listen to their calling and follow their dreams are the most successful people on our planet. They experience the type of success that is not just defined by how much money they have, but by how many people they help and the ways in which they change our world.

It's time for you to consciously create your vision, one that calls to you so strongly that you feel compelled to bring it to life. When you find the right vision for your business, it will literally become a magnet that pulls you forward. It will connect with your heart and soul so completely, that you will know at a profound level it is why you are on Earth.

As you consider the significant difference you are passionate to make, notice the starting place. It isn't how much money you make; it's how big of a *difference* you make. The money results from helping others.

Your big vision will help you become wealthy in three ways. First, it will *inspire you* to be motivated at higher levels. Second, it will *inspire others* to get on board to help bring your vision to life. Third, as others combine their energies and resources with yours, what was originally your vision becomes a *shared vision*. As more people share your vision, it will expand and create change faster. It can become a movement, one that transforms both others' lives and our world.

So, what is that heartfelt difference within you? What is your personal vision of how life can be different?

Perhaps you have a vision of how parents' lives can be easier, single mothers can make more money, or people can become healthier and find greater balance. You may have a message inside of you that you want to bring forth as a speaker, writer, coach, or expert.

Some people have visions of how to improve business, such as better ways to lead, build teams, market more effectively, close larger numbers of sales, or develop more efficient systems. Others want to create a healthy planet, sustainable lifestyles, and green products.

Whatever the heartfelt difference is within you, what-ever you are passionate to do with your life and business, the world needs you to bring your unique difference forward. As your coach, I am here to support you on your journey of waking up and hearing your calling. I am here to help you turn your *passions* into *profits*!

If you are beginning a new business, then creating your vision is the right place to start. If you currently own a business, then your renewed vision can help you redefine and energize your business purpose. The material in Chapter 4, *Passion, Purpose, and Values*, will help you to develop your vision further. Then in Chapter 12, *Develop Your Business Model*, you will learn how to turn your vision into a visionary purpose that propels your business forward—to help others and create profits.

> **Coaching:** Open your *Conscious Millionaire Journal.* Write whatever ideas come to you about differences you want to make. Take note of which ones touch your heart and excite you!

Expand Your Consciousness

To expand your consciousness is to move beyond your current way of viewing life. When you do, you see more of the opportunities and possibilities inherent in any situation. You also become aware of more ways to grow your business and make a difference.

> *Choose actions that will*
> *benefit you, others, and society.*

Begin expanding your perspective by considering that what others want and need are as important as your wants and needs. Think about the interactions between a business and a customer. Now, think about your own experiences as a customer.

As a customer, who would you prefer to do business with and why? Would you prefer to buy from someone who only cares about selling you their product or service? Or would you prefer to do business with someone who *genuinely cares* about you as a person and how they can help you; someone who is concerned about your major problems, aspirations, and what's in *your best interest?*

The answer is clear, isn't it? Just as it is equally obvious as to which approach would help you grow your business and profits. Put the problems and aspirations of your customers first. Be mindful of what matters to them.

> By expanding your consciousness, you become empowered to achieve and give more.

Now, extend this to the world and take a high level view of society's problems and how you can help solve them. Review the major trends and how the difference you want to make can be channeled to respond to them.

For example: Consider the trend of people seeking to live healthier lives. If you want to enhance the quality of others' health, think of the *conscious focused actions* you could take, such as providing healthier foods, education on how to live in healthier ways, and improvements you could make to the environment.

Expanding your consciousness involves moving from maintaining only one perspective, yours, to utilizing three conscious perspectives:

1. **Yourself:** including owners/entrepreneurs and investors/lenders;

2. **Others**: including customers, team, and suppliers;

3. **Society:** including your community and our environment.

When you move from focusing only on yourself to also looking at life from the perspective of others and society, your consciousness expands. By expanding your consciousness, you become empowered to achieve and give more. Moreover, you now see others and society as being partners with whom you are working to solve problems.

Many people find it helpful to think of society as their community. This can include the community in which you geographically live as well as the community of people in your profession or industry.

Another perspective is to think about society as being a cause you want to support. This can include an existing movement to which you want to contribute resources, as a participant or leader. It could also include a movement you desire to start. Further, society can also mean our *environment* or planet.

By thinking of society in these ways, you transition from conceptual ideas to specific actions that you can take to help our society and world become better.

Coaching: Open your *Conscious Millionaire Journal.* Describe what "community" means to you. Identify three ways you could help your community.

New Wealth Consciousness

As we move into the *Second Stage of Capitalism*™, we are experiencing a major shift in our consciousness about wealth. It is a shift away from the old view that for one person to win, another must lose, to a new view in which you, others, and society can all win simultaneously. I refer to this as a *Triple Win*™: win-win-win.

This *New Wealth Consciousness* is at the heart of *Conscious Millionaire*. It is based on a shift in nine beliefs. When you embrace these new beliefs, you experience a personal shift in your wealth consciousness; a shift both in how you view wealth and how you create it.

The following list contrasts nine beliefs of the old wealth consciousness with nine beliefs of the *New Wealth Consciousness*:

The Nine Belief Differences

Old Wealth Consciousness (win-lose)	New Wealth Consciousness (win-win-win)
scarcity, there is not enough	abundance, there is plenty
we are here to compete	we are here to collaborate
power through domination	power through cooperation
fear-based, inauthentic	heart-based, authentic
focus on past, rigid views	focus on future, possibilities
live by rules and authority	live in flow and synergy
there are limited choices	there are unlimited choices
we are separate beings	we are part of a united team
I win—others lose	you, others, society win together

When you live in the old wealth consciousness, you have a scarcity mindset. You don't believe there is enough money or resources to go around. This results in living in fear that you will never have enough. Your focus becomes how to out-compete others for customers, talent, and resources. You are constantly afraid you will lose everything and become bankrupt, so you actually restrict your business growth by being afraid to spend money on marketing and hiring top talent.

You falsely believe that for you to win, others must lose. This is because you not only think you are separate and essentially alone on your quest for wealth, you also believe there is a limited pool of wealth in the world. When you are in this old scarcity mindset, you believe real power comes from dominating, exploiting, and exerting authority over others. However, the truth is abundant wealth results from collaborating and working together for the common good—so you, others, and the world all win together.

You hold onto past, rigid ways of seeing life, because it feels safer. This causes you to live an inauthentic life, one in which you actually limit your own choices because you are afraid of being open to new possibilities. You feel alone, separate from others, and empty inside.

Instead of being conscious of your real power and how, by connecting to others you can become true partners, you continue to perpetuate inaccurate beliefs that neither serve you nor anyone else. Therefore, instead of cooperating with others to maximize both your and their wealth, you never achieve your true potential. You are afraid of being open and vulnerable.

You create wealth
by adding value to others!

However, *when you wake up* to what is truly possible in your life and shift to a *New Wealth Consciousness*, you realize that life is naturally abundant. There is actually no limit on the amount of wealth you can enjoy. The reason is simple. You can create an unlimited amount of wealth by adding value to others.

How do you add value? You start by making a difference to others in ways that matter to them. In this regard, your life becomes significant because you help others. It can come in the form of any product, service, or experience that solves your customers' problem or helps them fulfill a desire.

When you provide the value you are on Earth to deliver, you will have all the customers you could ever desire.

Because you can leverage how you create your difference, there is truly no limit as to how much wealth you, or anyone, can create.

Once you understand this, you naturally desire to build cooperative partnerships so you can leverage yourself. Rather than focusing on lack, fear, and how to out-compete others, your focus turns to expanding wealth, both for yourself and for those with whom you partner. You realize that you aren't here to compete, in the sense of crushing or putting your competition out of business, but to create new possibilities.

You move from thinking you are alone on your quest for wealth, and therefore must compete, to realizing that you are here to collaborate with others. You realize the profound thought that abundant wealth results from collaborating and working together for the common good. By doing so, you, others, and the world all win together.

When you effectively provide the value you are on Earth to deliver, you will have all the customers you could ever desire.

With this *New Wealth Consciousness,* you move into a heart-centered, authentic way of living and conducting business; one that supports a future that is right for you, others, and society at large. You feel connected to others and experience being part of a united team.

> There is actually no limit on the amount of wealth you can create.

You find that it is easy to become open to possibility and seek a natural flow to your life, one in which you regularly create synergies with others. You realize that you are always at conscious choice both as to how you create wealth and how much wealth you create. The more conscious you become, the more options and opportunities you naturally see.

Your entire world changes because you now view life differently. It is as if your blinders were removed and you see the abundant possibilities that exist in every moment.

When not only you, but the people in your business, family, friendships, organizations, and community also choose to make this shift in wealth consciousness, the world will begin to move into a new way of living and creating wealth.

As an entrepreneur on the Conscious Millionaire path, you are on the cutting edge of one of the biggest shifts that has ever occurred in how we see and create wealth.

> **Coaching:** Open your *Conscious Millionaire Journal.* Using the belief chart in this section, identify one old wealth belief that you may currently hold. List three ways you could grow your business by shifting it to the corresponding *New Wealth Consciousness* belief.

Conscious Focused Action Model

This is the second version of the foundational model, which is found in Chapter 2, *Formula for Creating Wealth.*

The conscious level and the focus level interrelate by utilizing each of the words on the conscious level with each focal point on the focus level. *For example:* Utilizing "others" (in this example, customers) from the focus level, ask:

- "What result will I help my *customers* achieve?" and, "Why is helping *customers* accomplish this result a priority?"

- "Who will benefit from *customers* achieving this result?" and, "Who will help *customers* attain this result?"

- "How can I best help *customers* reach this result?"

Note: In this example, helping customers clearly benefits them. Who else will benefit?

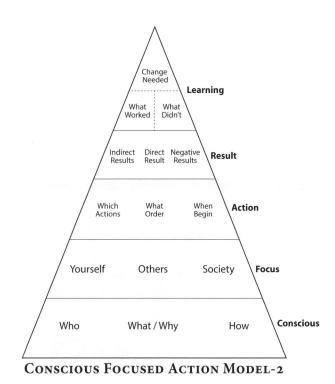

CONSCIOUS FOCUSED ACTION MODEL-2

Approach the other three levels—action, result, and learning—the same as in the foundational model. If you don't fully achieve your desired result, want to improve your process, or care to achieve your result at a higher level, then iterate. Review each level to determine what needs to change. Return to the conscious level and make the changes as you go through the model again. Then *test* the changes to determine if they are actually better.

CONSCIOUS MILLIONAIRE COACHING

Build Your Strategy

Open your *Conscious Millionaire Journal.* Write a three-step business strategy using *conscious focused action.* Develop your strategy utilizing the concept provided in the *conscious* step below. It is an important concept from this chapter.

1. Conscious: Create a goal of becoming aware of the best practices within your industry or profession. *For example:* "Read one business book a month and select best practices from it to apply to your business."

2. Focused: As you focus on your goal, choose three actions that will help you begin to achieve it. Determine the precise order for your actions.

3. Action: During the next twenty-four hours, execute by taking your three actions.

Grow Your Business

In your *Conscious Millionaire Journal* make notes on how you utilize each of the following to grow your business:

• Create a way in which your business can benefit your community and put it into action.

• Develop a message that shows you care about your customer. Utilize words that are meaningful to your customer. Discover these words by asking them.

• Design one strategy that simultaneously benefits your business, customer, and our society. Implement it.

Create Your Journey

Here are three choices for what to read next. The first is to read another *conscious* section. The second is to read another *millionaire* section. The third choice is to *journey* through the book linearly, reading it chapter by chapter.

continued

Conscious: Consider reading "Conscious Millionaire Leadership" section in Chapter 9, *Become a Conscious Leader*, before continuing to the next chapter.

Millionaire: Take a look at the "Develop Your Intuitive Edge" section in Chapter 7, *Your Millionaire Inner Zone*™, before going to the next chapter.

Journey: Continue forward to Chapter 4, *Passion, Purpose and Values*.

QR Codes / Links

Go the membership site to view a coaching video that reveals how to utilize the *New Wealth Consciousness* to grow and expand your business. Access the site now at:

ConsciousMillionaire.com/member

PASSION, PURPOSE, AND VALUES

*Turn your passion into profits
by helping others.*

In this chapter, you discover how passion ignites your
fire and helps you achieve your millionaire goals. Then you
will combine your passion, inner purpose, and strengths to
define your "true north." You will understand how purpose
provides a direction and learn how honesty and ethics help you
make more money. Then you will discover how to leverage your
passion, purpose, and values, to grow your wealth. In addition,
you will utilize the *Conscious Focused Action Model* to move
forward on your Conscious Millionaire Journey.

PASSION IGNITES YOUR FIRE

Imagine how much easier it will be for you to become a
millionaire if every day you are excited by your activities and the
results you are creating.

If you had unstoppable passion, would you get up early because you are more excited to be alive and eager to build your business? Would you move faster, jump higher, and do whatever it took to turn your biggest dreams into your new, vastly bigger reality?

Your biggest dreams are
expressions of your heart-passion.

Passion is what makes you excited, energized, and motivated to move forward. It's the fire in your belly. Without passion, your candle isn't even half lit. In fact, it is barely burning. As a result, you end up achieving little with your life or business. Worse, you don't feel alive; you're simply going through the motions.

Unfortunately, many of us begin losing our passion in childhood. We seek our parents' love and our teachers' approval. Equally important, we want to be liked and accepted by our friends and peer group. Because of this, most people give up part of themselves in exchange for becoming what is most acceptable to others.

We begin to think and behave the way *they* want. When we begin dating, we often give up part of who we are to please our boyfriend or girlfriend. As an adult, we relinquished more of our passion as we become caught up in the daily grind of working, as well as the responsibility of a home, family, and maintaining relationships.

Slowly, over time, we stop living a life that is totally real and passionate for us. Does this sound familiar?

As we begin to lose the deeper connection with ourselves, we literally fall out of touch with what it means to be authentic. Because our strongest experience of passion results from feeling real and alive, we begin to lose our inner fire; the inner fire that as a child made us naturally passionate and playful—the kind of fire that fueled our desire to dream big and believe that anything is possible.

Many people actually forget or never even realize what is most important to them. They lose touch with what fuels their deepest desire to become their best. Sometimes they are excited about what is going on at the surface of life. However, in order to feel your deepest levels of passion, to connect with your true self, you must dig deeper. You must connect with your heart and what feels real to you.

This is how you and I can best experience our passionate drive. Instead of endlessly pumping ourselves up with caffeine, drugs, and other stimulants, we can connect with our deepest passions. When this occurs, we tap into the energy source within us and become more alive and energetic.

The type of passion I'm discussing touches you to the core, my friend. It resonates with your very soul. It is the passion that makes you feel fully alive. When you feel this level of passion, you are fully present and easily absorbed in the here and now.

Passion Helps You Become a Millionaire

When you are building a business, your journey to becoming a millionaire is easier when fueled with a deep passion. If you are passionate about what you want to achieve, your drive translates into faster results and greater success. When you are doing things you are passionate about, you are also more fulfilled and therefore more eager to continue doing them.

The more passionate you are, the more easily you will attract other people. It's like you are magnetized and others are strongly attracted to you! Your energy flows out and connects with people around you. As your energy connects with them, they become attracted to you—and naturally feel drawn to you.

Like energy attracts like energy. This is why passionate people attract other passionate people. However, you also attract people who want to be like you. After all, everyone wants to possess abundant energy and feel more alive. The more passionate you become, the more you will attract others.

Because passion is energy in fast motion, passion is contagious. Therefore when you are passionate, you wake up the passionate feelings in others. Your fast moving, passionate energy can quickly energize a whole room. It can also energize your team and customers.

In your quest to create millionaire wealth, your passion helps move you forward to achieve your desired results. Think of the leaders you admire; are they passionless, cardboard-like people? Or, are they excited and focused on achieving something they are passionate about and believe in?

When your passion is heartfelt, you are tapping into an infinite spring of energy that flows from within you. This type of passion will give you energy and drive to take focused actions and achieve your millionaire dreams.

> **Coaching:** Open your *Conscious Millionaire Journal.* In it describe one or more passions that could help you become a millionaire. Identify how each passion could help you grow your business profits.

Purpose Gives You Direction

I believe we are each on this planet for a reason. Some people refer to it as their calling.

Your purpose is as much a part of who you are as is your gender, the color of your skin, or your physical size and attributes. It is part of the fabric of your being. Wherever you believe it came from, your purpose has always been a part of your *core nature.*

While we all have a specific purpose, until we become conscious of it, we are just taking a random walk down the street of life. There is no continuity between what you did yesterday, today, and will do tomorrow.

Here is the problem: Without a clear purpose—a specific difference you desire to make—you are like a ship lacking a rudder. You are headed in no particular direction. This isn't just true for your life, it is also true for your business. Purpose gives direction. It provides a focus.

Without a clear understanding of your purpose, you might try one way to make money this year. Then next year, you start a different type of business or decide to focus on an entirely different market. You routinely run off in many directions in hopes that some opportunity will finally be the "one" that will result in big money.

What's wrong with this picture? Without a clear direction and focus, you will likely waste a lot of energy. Instead of taking *conscious focused actions,* your efforts end up scattered in many directions. How can anyone achieve sustainable business success in this way?

However, when you begin to live "on purpose," when you apply your personal sense of purpose to how you make money, you have a clear direction for both your life and your millionaire journey. You also have a path to follow that gives you meaning.

Discover Your True North

Each of us is moving toward a future, one that we are sharing and jointly creating. What part do you feel called to play? What are you passionate to learn, experience, or achieve? What differences do you want to make? How do you want to use your personal strengths in your business and life? What is the massive value that you want to provide others and/or society? How do you want to make your community or our world a better place?

*Your true north is your path to
becoming a millionaire!*

There are three components to your *true north*: your *passion*, *purpose*, and *strengths*. While most people can easily discover their passion, it may take longer, and require digging deeper, to connect with your deeper purpose. One reason your passions are more easily accessible is they are expressions of strong emotions—feelings that you regularly experience.

By contrast, purpose resides deeper inside, at the core of your being, on what many people would call the soul level. Think of your true north as a gentle nudging from the deeper realms within as to why you were born and what you are on Earth to accomplish.

Uncovering your purpose is a discovery process. It may happen through a series of insights, or you may experience a single epiphany in which you achieve total clarity. By discovering my own purpose and working with clients, I found an easy way to uncover purpose: focus on the *difference* you desire to make in the world.

People who primarily view life as being logical, sometimes experience difficulty discovering their purpose. This is because, just like your passion, your purpose isn't mental. You don't think it; instead, you *feel it*. You feel your purpose deep within your heart and soul. This is why your passion and purpose are so strongly interrelated—you access both through your heart-centered feelings.

By completing the following three coaching exercises, you will begin to develop an understanding of your true north:

1. Heart-Passion: *What are your deepest passions?* These are the interests, hobbies, and activities you enjoy so much that when you engage in them, you easily become so absorbed that you lose all sense of time. We all have interests, such as food, music, and fun things to do that we love. However, your deeper passions touch your heart and bring a feeling of joy to your whole being.

Your deeper passions include areas such as: excelling in an activity you enjoy like a sport or something artistic or musical; learning; teaching; adventure; travel; and helping others achieve their goals. These passions raise your energy and make you feel more alive. They bring you so much joy that you never grow tired of doing them. Moreover, they also point you in the direction of your purpose.

> **Coaching:** Open your *Conscious Millionaire Journal* and list activities you are passionate about. Which of these make you feel the most excited? Which would you enjoy pursuing in a business? How motivated would you be to get up each morning to do these activities?

2. Inner Purpose: *What are the differences you want to make?* There is something you yearn to do. Perhaps it is a way in which you desire to help others improve their lives or excel at higher levels. Maybe you want to assist businesses or organizations to help them grow or operate more effectively. Perhaps you want to make a difference in your community or nation. Or you may feel a calling to help animals, our planet's environment, become involved in human rights initiatives, or support global causes.

Assuming anything is possible, fast forward to the final day of your life. You have enjoyed an amazingly fulfilled life because you have served and given in ways that mattered—both to you and others. Now imagine the difference you made. It was the difference your soul yearned to make, the true reason you are here on Earth. Consider how you can infuse this difference into your business. What was that difference?

Note: If you have difficulty discovering your purpose, use your strongest passions and your strengths to determine your true north. Then, at a later date, when your purpose becomes clear to you, add it into your true north. It will provide additional depth.

> **Coaching:** Open your *Conscious Millionaire Journal* and list the differences you feel a desire to make. Which ones call to you the strongest? Imagine one of these being *the* purpose for your business. If it were, how much more driven would you and your team become?

3. Core Strengths: *What are your natural strengths?* Most people have one or more strengths that come so easily that they do them almost perfectly every time. Think about your strengths, the gifts you received at birth. Your strengths may include ways in which you think, use your emotions, or are physically gifted

Your strengths are what you do well. Perhaps your mind naturally develops strategies, analyzes problems, invents novel ways to solve problems or creates new products. You may be caring and loving, easily relate to others emotionally, be intuitive, spiritual, or innately compassionate. You could be naturally athletic, skilled in a specific sport, or good at building with your hands. Perhaps you have an innate understanding of how to lead, mentor, or coach.

Whether you want to start a business or want to take an existing business in a new direction, one of the most effective ways to accomplish this is to incorporate one of your skill strengths into your business. Examples of how to do this include:

1. Coaching Strength: providing business coaching, offering weight loss coaching, or franchising children sports schools.

2. Cooking Strength: owning bakeries, developing a gourmet delivery service, or franchising an international restaurant chain.

3. Gardening Strength: building a lawn care service, owning a plant store, or having a landscape business.

4. Photography Strength: owning a pet photo studio, creating photography books, or offering wedding photography services.

5. Technology Strength: providing business mobility services, developing online games, or owning a cell phone repair business.

Your true north is an outward expression of your passion, sense of purpose, and natural strengths.

> **Coaching:** Open your *Conscious Millionaire Journal* and list your strengths that you naturally perform at a high level. If you had your dream business, which of these strengths would you utilize daily?

THE CONVERGENCE FACTOR

Identifying your true north is the first step to business success. Next, identify various options for how you could utilize your passion, purpose, and strengths to build products/services. Just know, *not* every option for expressing your true north will be profitable. Only options that provide what your customers' want, will create profits.

Your job as an entrepreneur is to bridge any gap that exists between how you express your true north and what your customers care about—the benefits they are eagerly seeking. Creating this bridge is what I call the *convergence factor*.

Now, the goal in doing this is never to abandon or even alter your true north. Rather, the goal is to discover how to utilize your true north to solve your customers' pressing problems or help them achieve their dream aspirations. To do this, create a

> The bigger the difference you make, the bigger the profit you can create.

bridge that connects the difference you care about with what your customers care about—bring the two together.

When you do this well, you can achieve amazing results, such as rapid business growth. How? By creating a powerful difference, one that matters to both you and your customers.

There are three components to creating a profitable convergence between your *true north* and what your customers will buy. The first component is the *true north* itself, which you identified in the prior section of this chapter.

The second component is the *offer* you make. While many entrepreneurs make the mistake of offering to sell the features of their products/services, the most profitable offers always focus on the *benefits*. These are all the ways your product/service adds value to your customers' lives, businesses, or organizations. Add terms, such as price, to your benefits to create a market offer.

$$true\ north + offer + buyer = profit$$

The third component to creating a convergence is a *buyer* who is ready and eager to purchase your offer. As you consider your offer and buyer, think of the money these can generate by coming together. Begin to equate money with the value, or difference, you make for your customers. In general, the bigger the difference you make, the bigger the profit you can create.

Identify Your Core Values

Your values are beliefs to which you associate strong, positive emotions. It is the combination of belief and strong emotion that turns a belief into a value. The longer you have held this association, the deeper and stronger are your values.

Values you hold the strongest are your core values. These are the guiding values of your life. They occur at an identity level. These values identify who you are and what is most important to you. They are often naturally compatible with your purpose statement. Expressing your core values supports you achieving your purpose—both in life and business.

These are the values that feel authentic and core to who you are as a person, leader, and entrepreneur. They answer questions such as, "What really matters in my life?" and, "Where should I lead my business?"

Whatever you identify as, "being me" is core to who you are and represents your strongest values. Just as your purpose resonates with your heart in a way that feels authentic for you, so do your core values.

values = belief + strong emotion

When your goals and actions are aligned with these values, you automatically put your whole heart into them. You will enjoy the most success when you utilize your strongest values to guide you in choosing the major goals for your life and business.

If you want your business to be an authentic expression of who you are, you will discover that your life and business values are consistent, if not similar. For instance, if being honest is something you value in personal relationships, you will likely value it in your business relationships as well.

Below is a list of values many people identify as most important:

honesty	profitability	family
integrity	accountability	friends
loyalty	mutual benefit	growth
respect	authenticity	freedom
efficiency	communication	spirituality

Coaching: Open your *Conscious Millionaire Journal.* List your top three to five business values. Think of values as the behaviors that will help grow your business.

Honesty, Ethics and Business Success

With whom would you prefer to do business? Someone who is honest with you and has integrity, or someone you consider dishonest, unethical, and you don't trust? The answer is simple, isn't it? The same is true for your prospects, clients, and customers.

This extends to the relationships you build with your employees, suppliers, contractors, business alliances, and strategic partners. It actually applies to anyone with whom you relate through your business.

Honesty begins with keeping your word, which is a commitment you give to both yourself and others. To be honest, you must first become conscious of what is actually true for you. Then you must consciously communicate it to yourself and others.

By consciously choosing actions that are consistent with your word, you are acting with integrity. Your word and your actions are in sync with one another. Every time you keep your word, you build trust—first with yourself, second with others, and third with the community in which your business operates. But how does honesty relate to ethics? Why are ethics so important to your level of business and financial success?

*Your ethics communicate what
others can consistently rely on from you.*

Think of ethics as your standard of behavior. These are the standards for how you conduct yourself and how you expect others to behave. Your business ethics reflect the type of actions you find either acceptable or offensive. Do not let others or your environment change them.

When you express your standards to the world, you are giving *your word* this is what others can expect from you and your business. You are creating an expectation in their mind.

Every time you practice your standards, you are acting in the way you have defined as honest and ethical. You build trust and increase your customers' loyalty. This results in their doing more business with you which increases your wealth. It also often results in their becoming a *raving fan* that frequently refers their friends and associates to your business.

However, anytime you break your standards or fail to keep your word, you damage others' trust in you or your business. You hurt your relationship with them and decrease their desire to do business with you. As you probably already know, a disgruntled customer can rapidly spread their dissatisfaction through word-of-mouth and social media. Few things can more quickly hurt your business reputation and profits.

Coaching: Open your *Conscious Millionaire Journal* and write a list of behaviors that you want others to depend on and expect from your business. Choose three of these and write a short statement of your *ethical standards*.

Leverage Your Passion, Purpose, And Values

Think of your passion, purpose, and strongest values as *capital assets.* When it comes to creating wealth and becoming a millionaire, they are three of your most important assets. Why?

First, when you express your passionate purpose and act in accordance with your true values, you are tapping into your own natural motivators. This compels you to take action and move your business forward.

Second, they are assets because they identify who you are in the marketplace. They are the most important elements of your business brands. They communicate what you value and the specific difference you promise to create for your customers. In marketing terms, they set you apart and differentiate you from other businesses.

Third, when you use them in your marketing, they resonate with the type of prospect ideally suited to become your customer. This is because your message is relevant to them and what they seek. It connects with what they value.

Equally important, they are who *you will most enjoy* as clients because they naturally want what you and your business are all about. They want, and probably need, what you are on Earth to provide.

When you build your business by making a positive difference to those you feel passionately motivated to help, it is easier for you to make money and also experience your deepest levels of fulfillment.

Your passion, purpose, and values are three of your most *precious capital assets.* Treasure them. They are why you are here on Earth and should be primary reasons you are in business.

Leverage these assets by making them core to how you do business. Utilize them to create your business vision and develop your products and services. Bring them into your marketing so you attract the right customers. Your passion, purpose, and values provide direction on your path to becoming a Conscious Millionaire.

Conscious Focused Action Model

This is the third version of the foundational model, which is found in Chapter 2, *Formula for Creating Wealth.*

The conscious level and focus level interrelate by utilizing each of the words on the conscious level with each focal point on the focus level. *For example:* utilizing "passion" from the focus level, ask:

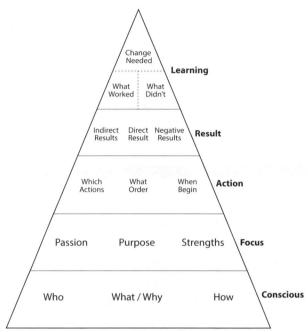

CONSCIOUS FOCUSED ACTION MODEL-3

• "Who will benefit from my using *passion* to achieve this result?" and, "Who will help me become *passionate* so I can attain the result?"

• "What result will I use *passion* to achieve?" and, "Why is using *passion* to accomplish the result a priority?"

• "How do I best utilize *passion* to reach the desired result?"

Approach the other three levels—action, result, and learning—the same as in the foundational model. If you didn't fully achieve your desired result, want to improve your process, or care to achieve your result at a higher level, then iterate. Review each level to determine what needs to change. Return to the conscious level and make the changes as you go through the model again. Then *test* the changes to determine if they are actually better.

CONSCIOUS MILLIONAIRE COACHING

Build Your Strategy

Open your *Conscious Millionaire Journal*. Write a three-step business strategy using *conscious focused action*. Develop your strategy utilizing the concept provided in the *conscious* step below. It is an important concept from this chapter.

1. Conscious: Select one of the core values you chose for your business. Develop a goal of utilizing this value to help grow your business. *For example*: "We value honesty and will be honest with everyone with whom we do business."

2. Focused: As you focus on your goal, choose three actions that will help you begin to achieve it. Determine the precise order for your actions.

3. Action: During the next twenty-four hours, execute by taking your three actions.

Grow Your Business

In your *Conscious Millionaire Journal* make notes on how you utilize each of the following to grow your business:

• Define a purpose for your business that expresses the difference you want to achieve.

• Select your top three to five business values. Communicate them to your team, customers, and suppliers.

• Choose one way you could leverage your strengths to grow your business; then implement it.

Create Your Journey

Here are three choices for what to read next. The first choice is to read another *conscious* section. The second choice is to read another *millionaire* section. The third choice is to *journey* through the book linearly, reading it chapter by chapter.

continued

Conscious: Consider reading the "Develop Your Visionary Purpose" section in Chapter 9, *Become a Conscious Leader,* before continuing to the next chapter.

Millionaire: Take a look at the "Money-Purpose Wound" in Chapter 8, *Create an Abundance Mindset,* before going to the next chapter.

Journey: Continue forward to Chapter 5, *Conscious Millionaire Habits.*

QR Codes / Links

Go the membership site to view a coaching video that discusses how to discover your *true north.* Access the site now at:

ConsciousMillionaire.com/member

CONSCIOUS MILLIONAIRE HABITS

*You become your habits and
your habits become you.*

In this chapter, you learn how to become aware of your habits and how your habits are "unconscious patterns" that influence your business, finances, and life. You will be introduced to the seven *Conscious Millionaire Habits* and begin to use them to achieve greater business and financial success. These habits include "do what's right," which is one of the keys to consciously building your business. You will discover how to leverage your results daily. You will also learn a simple yet powerful, three-step technique for developing new habits. In addition, you will utilize the *Conscious Focused Action Model* to move forward on your Conscious Millionaire Journey.

How Habits Influence Your Wealth

Anything that you do on a repeated basis is a habit. They are so automatic, that you typically do them with no real awareness. When you stop to consider this, most of what you do throughout your business day is based on habits. This includes repeated ways you think, feel, or act.

Habits are actually *unconscious patterns* that are either moving you toward your goals (positive habits) or away from your goals (negative habits).

> Until you become conscious of your habits, they control you and your financial destiny.

Until you become conscious of your habits, they control you and your financial destiny. However, the moment you make a conscious decision to choose which to develop, you take control over your habits and your financial destiny.

For example: Consciously choosing to repeat positive internal statements such as, "I can achieve it," creates a positive *mental* habit. Choosing to repeatedly focus on a positive emotion, like confidence, creates a positive *emotional* habit. Repeatedly choosing to take an action, perhaps starting to work at 8 A.M., creates a *behavioral* habit.

Any repeated way you think, feel, or act that helps you take steps forward toward achieving financial and business success is a millionaire success habit.

Your habits influence
every aspect of your future.

How you approach your business day, the mindset you develop, and the financial success you achieve are all influenced, and to a large degree determined, by the habits you develop.

To understand how habits work, think of a pool of water. Now, imagine that several rocks are dropped into the middle of the pool. A number of ripples, all moving outward from the center, would work together to create a wave. Because the ripples are aligned, they move together in an outward direction.

The same thing occurs when you have a large number of positive habits. They all work together to create a *big wave of positive energy* that moves you toward your desired result.

By contrast, think of your negative habits as rocks that are dropped in the water *outside the center* of the pool. They create ripples that move *against* and interfere with the positive, outward moving waves. The negative ripples work to slow the positive ripples from moving forward.

This is also what occurs when you have negative habits. They work against your positive habits. They interfere with you achieving the success you desire.

Your goal is to establish such a strong set of positive habits that instead of being just ripples, they become a massive wave of energy that moves you toward success. By developing a big wave of positive habits, you create a massive force of positive energy that moves you forward through your business day.

> **Coaching:** Open your *Conscious Millionaire Journal.* Write a financial goal for your business, one that you want to achieve within three months. List at least three positive habits that would help you achieve your goal. Visualize them as part of a big wave of positive habits that support the achievement of your goal.

CONSCIOUS MILLIONAIRE HABITS

By developing the seven *Conscious Millionaire Habits,* you create the behavioral patterns that will help you build a business, one that both achieves a greater good and creates high profits. The first three habits are based on the *Formula for Creating*

Wealth: make *conscious choices*, develop laser focus, and take fast actions. These three habits provide a strong foundation for you achieving predictable entrepreneurial success.

While it is important for your success that you develop all seven of these habits, if you attempt to develop all seven at one time, you will probably feel overwhelmed. When it comes to learning something new, such as developing a new habit, it is critical to focus on small chunks, one at a time.

Realize that anything you do on a repeated basis is a habit. So, learning a habit is really learning to repeat the same thoughts, feelings, or behaviors.

Instead of attempting to develop all seven habits at one time, choose one of the habits by applying it in your business and financial life every day for the next thirty days. Then next month, choose another habit to learn. In only seven months, you will have both developed and incorporated all seven habits into your life. As a result, you will be in a position to create an enormous wave of positive energy; one that propels you toward increasing business and financial success.

CM HABIT 1: MAKE CONSCIOUS CHOICES

Entrepreneurs who become financially successful and make the greatest contributions to our world make conscious choices. They understand the importance of consciously choosing their business vision, model, goals, strategies, and actions. They are aware of and carefully analyze each of their options. Then they choose those options that are most aligned with their values, overall priorities, and risk tolerance.

These new *entrepreneurs* connect with higher consciousness and create purposeful visions of the change they want to make in their clients' lives. They make choices that align with and support achieving the purpose they have chosen to guide their business.

When you make conscious choices, you make an intentional decision to take control over your business and financial destiny. You become conscious of the many possibilities for your business then choose the ones you most desire. You become aware of the actions that will most help you to reach your outcomes; then consciously choose the best time and best way to implement them.

> Consider how your choices affect the lives your business touches, such as employees, customers, and people in your community.

Conscious choices are a *precondition* of every *important success* you will ever achieve in your business, finances, or personal life. This is because when you make conscious choices you consider the consequences of your decisions, both now and in the future. You consider both the positive and negative aspects of those consequences, as well as how today's choices will impact your business next week and the following year.

Consider how your choices affect the lives your business touches, such as employees, customers, and the people in your community. You see these aspects through the realization that your business is interconnected with theirs in ways that mean your destinies are interwoven. You realize that you will each win more by winning together.

Be aware there is no such thing as an unimportant choice or small decision. This is true because each choice creates ripples. These ripples affect not only the options you will have in your future, but the options *others* will have as well.

The problem is that many entrepreneurs attempt to build their business without allowing time to consciously reflect on their choices. Instead, they simply take action without first consciously determining which option would create the best result. To maximize your success, consciously reflect on your choices *before* you take action.

Becoming a financially successful entrepreneur and making a powerful difference requires you to consciously choose your thoughts, feelings, and behaviors. This includes choosing to develop the habits that support your business growth. Conscious Millionaires develop the habit of making conscious choices, ones that support their business purpose, values, and goals.

CM Habit 2: Develop Laser Focus

Entrepreneurs who build high-growth businesses and make a positive difference with their lives, do so by developing and maintaining laser focus. They realize focus is power, because it keeps them on track so they don't become distracted by time-wasting activities. By focusing intently, they become more productive and effective as business owners and leaders. When you develop laser focus, you become a powerful force that can cut through any barrier that exists between you and what you desire.

For example: When you focus on a goal, your thoughts, emotions, and actions all become aligned with accomplishing it. As this occurs, you enter a zone in which you seem to know automatically what to do in order to reach your desired outcome.

Focus is a *precondition* of every *important success* you will ever achieve in your business, finances, or personal life. This is because when you focus on a specific result, you move energy into it. And as you do, you also attract energy from your environment. This energy comes to you in the form of ideas and resources that support you in achieving your best outcome.

> When you develop laser focus, you become a powerful force that can cut through any barrier

In addition, many people are attracted to those who have energy that is laser-focused. Becoming focused creates a charisma that attracts others like a magnet. When a group of people focus together on a single outcome, they build a powerful momentum that quickly moves them toward that goal.

Simply, entrepreneurs who create the fastest growth and achieve the greatest good for their clients and society are the most focused. Those who underachieve, are the least focused. Highly focused entrepreneurs routinely achieve several times what unfocused business owners achieve—in the same twenty-four hours. Why?

When you develop laser focus, you become a powerful force that can cut through any barrier that exists between you and what you desire.

The more productive entrepreneurs are conscious of their top priorities and focus all of their actions on achieving them. They remain focused on whatever is the highest and best use of their time. They stay focused and *follow through* until they reach completion. Conscious Millionaires develop the habit of laser focus.

CM Habit 3: Take Fast Action

Entrepreneurs who build the largest companies, make the most money, and create the greatest positive change for their clients and society, consistently take fast actions. They understand this secret: *success loves action and rewards speed*. Successful entrepreneurs apply this secret daily by choosing the results they want, and rapidly taking action to reach them.

When you take fast action, you build momentum. It takes less energy to continue moving forward than it did to initially create the momentum. It can take five times the energy to start your momentum than it does to keep it in motion. Entrepreneurs who make millions know this. They have learned to stay focused and continue taking action once they have energy moving in the right direction.

Provided you consciously choose your direction and are focused on the right actions, the entrepreneur who takes fast action usually wins the biggest. Consider this for a moment: Who usually builds the most profitable company? It is the entrepreneur who is first to market with a new idea and then continually executes by taking action to build momentum. Why? To attract customers, media attention, and claim the market.

Fast action is a *precondition* of every *important success* you will ever achieve in your business and financial life. This is because when you take fast action you get fast results. Some of these results are spot-on with what you wanted; others are not.

Moreover, fast results provide you with fast feedback. Instead of taking months to determine if your actions are achieving your desired result, you will know in days or weeks. This empowers you to adjust your actions, so you remain on track to achieve your desired result.

In addition, you are able to build upon your rapidly achieved results. They become your new foundation to create business growth, develop new products and services, and adjust your business model and success plan to quickly expand your business.

Entrepreneurs who struggle in their businesses are often the same people who procrastinate. Because they wait rather than acting quickly on their ideas, they miss their real opportunities, fail to achieve their goals, and accomplish far less than the entrepreneurs who act quickly. Conscious Millionaires develop the habit of taking fast action.

CM Habit 4: Do What's Right

Doing what's right serves the higher purpose; the difference you commit to making through your business. Cultivating this habit is an investment of your time, energy, and money, as well as emotional and spiritual potential. This habit will pay dividends to your business, customers, and all the other stakeholders associated with your business.

Doing what's right is a *precondition* to every *important success* you will ever achieve in your business, finances, or personal life. First, it is a commitment to make your behaviors consistent with your values. Second, it is a commitment to habitually keep your promises, beginning with the overall brand promise you select and communicate about your business.

> When you do what's right, it not only serves your business now, but over the long term.

Third, it is a commitment to build a culture of doing what's right 100 percent of the time. Make all your behaviors completely congruent with what you promise to others and say you value.

Developing trust, familiarity, and predictability in the minds of your customers results from your team always doing what's right. Customers need ways to differentiate your business from others. One important way is to differentiate your brand by doing what's right. This can include: building products designed to benefit them; not harming the environment in how you conduct business; and handling disputes in a manner that serves your customers and upholds your stated values.

Consciousness and business combine to create a common good. This is never more exhibited than when your business policies, practices, and procedures naturally lead to your people always doing what's right. It will generate greater respect for your brand, enhance your credibility with your ideal customer, and result in a positive word of mouth about your business. This is free marketing of the type money can't buy.

Doing what's right serves your business both now and over the long term. When you integrate doing what's right with a long-term perspective, you open up new potentials for the value you can bring our world. This includes your business growing into a larger, highly-profitable enterprise that will reach forward in time to benefit people who are not yet even born.

> *Doing what's right*
> *adds credibility to your brand.*

As you develop your visionary purpose, think three, five, even ten years into the future. Ask yourself how doing the right thing and taking the right actions will affect the future of your business and finances.

How will doing what's right attract more opportunities? How will it help you attract the people that you want to associate with your brand? Developing this habit will increase your possibilities for making money, helping others, and creating your desired difference.

Establish your business as a model of what it means to "do what's right." Demonstrate it in all that you say, the decisions you make, and how you act in every situation. Conscious Millionaires develop the habit of doing what's right.

> **Coaching:** Open your *Conscious Millionaire Journal.* Describe what it means to always do what is right in your customer relationships. List five to ten exemplary actions you want your team members to routinely take with each customer.

CM Habit 5: Leverage Yourself Daily

Leverage is a form of multiplication. Entrepreneurs who create a massive difference and achieve lasting business growth use leverage daily to multiply their business and expand their reach. They understand that leverage is a means to grow their business exponentially. Without leverage, they would limit their accomplishments and goals.

Conscious Millionaires use leverage to multiply their results in ways that are for their own good, the good of others, and the good of society. They utilize leverage to channel what is in their heart into a massive difference increases their business growth and profits. Through leverage, they increase the benefits to everyone their business touches.

When you use leverage, you develop ways to reach more people with the same or even less effort. You tap into a power that every major corporation understands. As an entrepreneur, you must utilize the power of leverage if you want to make millions. There are six major ways in which you can leverage: (1) time, (2) money, (3) resources, (4) skills and knowledge, (5) your network, and (6) automating systems.

Leverage your results daily!

By applying a fulcrum to a rock, you can easily move a heavy boulder, which you otherwise couldn't budge. Imagine how much greater results you could achieve in your business by using leverage.

Leverage is a *precondition* of every *important success* you will ever achieve in your business, finances, or personal life. This is because when you leverage, you multiply your results exponentially. By leveraging time, money, resources, skills and knowledge, your network, and automating systems, you can magnify your positive results and outcomes.

One of the fastest ways to leverage is through systems automation. *For example*: You can utilize software to set up your email sequences and marketing. This leverages time because you can set up the email sequence once and it goes to thousands—even millions—of people.

Therefore, automate much of your marketing, selling, and delivery of products. Automation leverages money. *For example:* You pay for the copywriting in emails or the cost of producing videos once. However, by using automation, you can send them to many people for one cost.

In addition, automation leverages *resources* (purchase or license one software program, yet use it to sell to many people), as well as *skills* and *knowledge* (by using skills only once, such as to create a sequence of emails that delivers your information to everyone in your audience at once). You could also leverage your contacts by partnering with the people you know, so they send out *your* emails to *their* lists.

Conscious Millionaires develop the habit of leveraging themselves *daily*. They multiply their results in ways that are for their good, the good of others, and the good of society as well.

> **Coaching:** Open your *Conscious Millionaire Journal*. Identify one way you could use leverage to grow your business. Choose three *conscious focused actions* that would help you leverage in this way. Take these actions during the next twenty-four hours.

CM HABIT 6: SEEK OPPORTUNITIES

Entrepreneurs who achieve the greatest success, constantly and consistently seek new opportunities. They understand the importance of generating a pipeline of opportunities that can provide new channels of revenue. They also realize that some of their biggest breakthroughs occur by incorporating new opportunities into their business model.

When you discover new opportunities, you unlock a powerful source of new potential for your business. However, in order to determine which opportunities are right for you and your business, first develop a clear business purpose, goals, and values. Then use these as part of your criteria for identifying the best opportunities for your business.

> Successful entrepreneurs allow time to seek new opportunities weekly.

Seeking opportunities is a *precondition* of every *important success* you will ever achieve in your business and finances. To effectively seek opportunities, laser focus on what you want and become open to discovering new ways to achieve it. Expand the potential ways to build and grow your business by introducing new ideas and possibilities into your business.

Successful entrepreneurs allow time to seek opportunities weekly. Before they begin their search, they develop a short, precise list of criteria that describes the type of opportunities they desire. Then they review each opportunity by comparing it to their criteria.

These criteria include the results the entrepreneur seeks. *For example*: How to solve a current problem, provide a new avenue for acquiring customers, increase the difference they make, and help society. The criteria also includes how well an opportunity *fits* with their business purpose, goals, and values. Throughout the day, they keep an eye out for possible opportunities.

With their criteria in mind, successful entrepreneurs constantly seek opportunity leads. *For example*: Information on billboards, and news items on radio, TV, and the Internet. They pay attention to what stands out as a possible lead for an opportunity, including what is said in conversations. They also develop a list of referral partners—people they know as friends or business associates—and check with them on a regular basis to determine if they know of any opportunities that fit their criteria.

Then once a week, they meet with their team or coach to review potential opportunities. They compare their potential opportunities against their criteria, short-term goals, and long-term goals. In addition, they evaluate both the potential ROI and the risks associated with each opportunity. Conscious Millionaires grow their businesses by developing the habit of seeking opportunities.

> **Coaching:** Open your *Conscious Millionaire Journal.* Describe one type of opportunity that would help grow your business. Select three *conscious focused actions* you can take during the next twenty-four hours to discover this type of opportunity. Take the actions.

CM Habit 7: Learn and Grow

Entrepreneurs who build high-profit businesses as well as meaningful, rewarding lives, are constantly learning and growing. They are life-long learners who consistently seek to acquire new knowledge and develop new skills. They are committed to growing, both professionally and personally, by consciously choosing experiences that require them to stretch beyond their comfort zone.

When you learn and grow, you expand the possibilities for your business, finances, and personal life. Further, if you want to grow your business, increase profits, and make a significant difference, then you have to study how to make money. You need to achieve wealth mastery.

Also learn what matters most to your customer, what problems the world has that you may be able to solve, and stay current on technology that can help you achieve your outcomes.

Attend wealth conferences, business trainings, and develop a mentoring or coaching relationship with someone who has already achieved the level of success you seek.

Learning and growing are *preconditions* for every *important success* you will ever achieve in your business, finances, or personal life. The only way you can quickly attain the results you want, is to learn what is and isn't working. Then adjust your strategies and take new actions. Learning is the highest level in the Consci*ous Focused Action Model.* It is highest because it is where real conscious change begins.

Conscious Millionaires make it a priority to invest in themselves and their team. They realize that exposing themselves to new ideas, strategies, and models of excellence provides them with a strong advantage. Likewise, they understand the value it brings to their business to invest in their team members. They realize that by providing opportunities for their people to grow, they are laying the foundation for their business to grow as well.

Instead of wasting time watching television, they invest in themselves by constantly reading business and personal success books, articles, and magazines. They invest in becoming a great leader and entrepreneur by attending leadership conferences. They utilize online and home-study programs as well as audio and video trainings to constantly develop and expand their entrepreneurial skills.

Over the course of my life to date, I have already invested more than $350,000 in attaining educational degrees as well as attending business success trainings, conferences, and workshops. My investment includes home-study programs, books, audio programs, private and group coaching, master-

> Conscious Millionaires make it a priority to invest in themselves and their team.

minds, and resource materials, such as paying for access to motivating membership sites.

Also, I nurture and develop my inner life by attending personal, spiritual, and consciousness-related conferences and events. I focus on my growth by regularly meditating, practicing Qigong, reading, listening to inspiring audio programs, and watching videos that expand my consciousness. These are some of the ways in which I personally invest in my learning and growth.

So, as your coach, I invite you to consider what investments you will make over the next twelve months in your personal, financial, and entrepreneurial learning and growth. What is your personal and professional growth worth to you?

As a business coach, mentor, and advisor, I consistently find that all entrepreneurs who achieve at their highest level, invest in their skills and future. They attend conferences and boot camps, attend webinars, join mastermind groups, and read books.

They also invest in themselves by hiring a skilled business coach to help them refine their strategies, create a wealth mindset, and stay accountable. Like all top entrepreneurs, Conscious Millionaires develop the habit of constantly learning and growing.

> **Coaching:** Open your *Conscious Millionaire Journal.* List five *conscious focused actions* you will take to help you learn and grow over the next twelve months. These might include: reading a business book each month; attending business skills webinars; listening to success audios; attending entrepreneur trainings; hiring a business coach; or joining a mastermind.

How to Develop a New Habit

Use this simple, three-step technique to develop a new habit in as few as thirty days.

1. Identify the Habit: Choose a new habit you want to develop. *For example:* Develop laser focus.

2. Create a "Big Why": Make two lists. First, list what it will cost you, others, and society if you do *not* develop the new habit. Consider the *emotional pain* of keeping your business or life as they are now. Second, list all the ways that you, others, and society will *benefit* by you developing the new habit. Consider the *emotional pleasure* of having the new habit.

For example: The *costs* to yourself, others, and society of not developing laser focus might include a scattered state of mind so you miss deadlines, fail to close enough sales, and go into debt. This could result in the gut wrenching experience of your business failing, losing your car and home, and not having the money to send your children to college. Further, you wouldn't have money to help causes you care about or be in a position to generously give to others.

The *benefits* of developing laser focus for yourself, others, and society, could include: closing more sales, growing a bigger business, creating more profit, and making a larger difference to your clients. You could also afford memorable family vacations and establish the funds needed to send your children to college. Further, you would generate the money necessary to support causes in which you believe and give to others who need your help.

Note: The *secret* to creating a "big why" is choosing reasons that have strong emotional charges for you (both negative costs and positive benefits). Think of these as your level 10 feelings.

3. Define and Repeat the Habit: Define the thought, emotion, and action components of this habit. Then repeat each of them on a daily basis in a way that benefits your business and life. *For example:* You think, "stay focused on target"; you feel "unstoppable"; and you "take action steps" that move you toward your chosen result.

> **Coaching:** Open your *Conscious Millionaire Journal.* Choose one of the seven Conscious Millionaire Habits and describe how you will utilize the above technique to develop this habit during the next thirty days. Make a commitment to developing it.

CONSCIOUS FOCUSED ACTION MODEL

CONSCIOUS FOCUSED ACTION MODEL - 4

This is the fourth version of the foundational model, which is found in Chapter 2, *Formula for Creating Wealth*.

The top tier and bottom tier of the conscious level interrelate by utilizing each of the *habits* on the top tier with each of the words on the bottom tier. *For example:* Utilizing the "*do what's right*" habit from the top tier, ask:

- "What result will *doing what's right* help achieve?" and, "Why is *doing what's right* to accomplish this result a priority?"

- "Who will benefit from my *doing what's right* to achieve this result?" and, "Who will help *do what's right* to attain this result?"

- "How can I best *do what's right* to reach this result?"

At the focus level, consider each of the three conscious perspectives: *yourself*, *others*, and *society*. These are the options for those who will benefit.

Approach the other three levels—action, result, and learning—the same as in the foundational model. If you don't fully achieve your desired result, want to improve your process, or care to achieve your result at a higher level, then iterate. Review each level to determine what needs to change. Return to the conscious level and make the changes as you go through the model again. Then *test* the changes to determine if they are actually better.

CONSCIOUS MILLIONAIRE COACHING

Build Your Strategy

Open your *Conscious Millionaire Journal*. Write a three-step business strategy using *conscious focused action*. Develop your strategy utilizing the concept provided in the *conscious* step below. It is an important concept from this chapter.

1. Conscious: Create a goal for incorporating the habit "do what's right" into how you make business decisions. *For example:* "Always do what's right when customer complaints or problems occur."

2. Focused: As you focus on your goal, choose three actions that will help you begin to achieve it. Determine the precise order for your actions.

3. Action: During the next twenty-four hours, execute by taking your three actions.

Grow Your Business

In your *Conscious Millionaire Journal* make notes on how you utilize each of the following to grow your business:

• Identify a negative habit that is holding you back from making more profits. Replace it with the opposite positive habit.

• Select a high priority goal for *today* and become 100 percent committed to achieving it. Stay focused on your goal until you complete it.

• Develop a list of criteria that defines your ideal opportunities. Over the next seven days, discover at least one opportunity that meets your criteria each day.

Create Your Journey

Here are three choices for what to read next. The first is to read another *conscious* section. The second is to read another *millionaire* section. The third choice is to *journey* through the book linearly, reading it chapter by chapter.

Conscious: Consider reading "The Power of Synchronicity" section in Chapter 7, *Your Millionaire Inner Zone*, before continuing to the next chapter.

Millionaire: Take a look at the "Mindset of Highly Successful Entrepreneurs" section in Chapter 8, *Create an Abundance Mindset*, before going to the next chapter.

Journey: Continue forward to Chapter 6, *Maximize Your Results Daily*.

QR Codes / Links

Go to the membership site to view a coaching video that reveals how to use leverage to achieve fast business growth. Access the site now at:

ConsciousMillionaire.com/member

MAXIMIZE YOUR RESULTS DAILY

There is no lack of time,
only lack of focus and organization.

In this chapter, you learn a structure for maximizing your results each day. You will establish your own millionaire standard and begin to develop millionaire confidence. Also, you will learn how to consciously create your day and achieve each of your top priorities. Then you will discover how to best use your evening to revitalize and prepare for another powerful day tomorrow. In addition, you will utilize the *Conscious Focused Action Model* to move forward on your Conscious Millionaire Journey.

YOUR MILLIONAIRE STANDARD

If you want to become a Conscious Millionaire, then become results focused. Moreover, to grow and expand your business, you must become committed to creating millionaire success days.

However, until you have a *standard* to use for evaluating your day, how would you know if your day is successful? The obvious answer is—you wouldn't know.

Here's the problem. Most people have no standard for their day, no standard for their actions, and no standard for their results. They do not create a standard for their business activities or daily life. Without a standard, there is no way to measure your success. Conscious Millionaires establish a results standard and use it daily.

They apply it to hold themselves accountable and evaluate their success. It is one of the reasons they perform higher and make more money than most people.

Your millionaire standard
helps you create more wealth faster!

Think of your millionaire standard as a benchmark, a measurement you can establish to evaluate your actions and results. It is your definition of the level at which you will keep your commitments and reach your results.

For your standard to have value, it must be *precise, concrete*, and *clear*. There must be no question in your mind, or anyone to whom you communicate the standard, as to what it is and how it can measure your results.

There are three standards. One of these will be right for the type of work you are doing on any day. Further, choose one to become your usual standard; the one you utilize most days. Each standard assumes you will perform quality work and achieve your best within the standard you have chosen.

1. Time based: Stay *100 percent focused* on specific actions and targeted results for a pre-established *period of time.* The standard is staying focused and only executing actions that move you toward your agreed results; not whether you fully achieve the result during the period of time. *For example:* Choose one result and stay 100 percent focused for sixty minutes on achieving it. During the time period, only take actions designed to achieve your desired result. Notice how much you achieve by staying laser-focused for a set time period.

2. Results based: Achieve each of the agreed actions and results by a targeted deadline, unless events beyond your *direct* control, hinder your progress. You agree to hold yourself accountable for any other situation and for achieving your commitments. *For example*: Choose one result to complete today and the actions necessary to achieve it. Hold yourself accountable to completely achieve your result today, unless events beyond your direct control occur that prevent you, such as: an unforeseeable traffic accident or a family emergency. By contrast, double-booking appointments is within your control and never a valid excuse.

3. No excuses: Choose the *quality level* of your performance and the *time frame* for achieving your agreed actions and results; then achieve them no matter what occurs. This is acting without any safety nets—there are no allowable excuses. *For example*: Choose a quality level of "no errors" and that you will achieve your result by 5 P.M. today. Even if you need to work at twice your regular pace or find additional people to help you complete the work, you will finish by 5 P.M. today—*NO EXCUSES.*

Most people find the first two standards work best for the majority of their activities and results. When they are working on a specific project that has a tight deadline, they use the third standard, and for a short period of time go all-out with no excuses.

> **Coaching:** Open your *Conscious Millionaire Journal.* Choose which *millionaire standard* you will utilize as your base standard. Describe how you will apply it to your commitments and actions. If you work with a team, also develop a "team standard" that is utilized when working together.

Conscious Millionaire Confidence

We all have fears: those internal feelings that act as emotional roadblocks. They stop us from achieving what we want. What is the best way to replace these negative feelings by building Conscious Millionaire confidence? By achieving one successful *conscious focused action* after another.

> *Develop Conscious Millionaire confidence by taking one successful action after another.*

Even one small, successful action that you acknowledge and celebrate will increase your confidence. The more confident you become, the more willing you are to venture outside of your current comfort zone. As you do, you will find it easier to set higher goals and take the actions necessary to achieve them. Why?

Each time your confidence increases, your internal beliefs and mindset change about what you are capable of accomplishing. As this occurs, you expand your zone of confidence and this influences how you show up in life—and what you accomplish. The more you grow your confidence, the faster you will grow your business profits and make your difference.

The more confidence you develop, the more you replace negative internal chatter with positive internal dialogue. Your negative self-talk about just getting by, not being good enough, and feeling like a failure, gives way to positive statements, such as: "I deserve to achieve more"; "I will succeed"; and "Deals are coming my way quickly." The more your confidence grows, the faster you will grow your business.

> **Coaching:** Open your *Conscious Millionaire Journal*. Keep a list of each successful *conscious focused action* you take during the next twenty-four hours. Note how each action helped develop your millionaire confidence.

Conscious Millionaire Daily Plan

Unsuccessful entrepreneurs allow their day to unfold in a haphazard manner. However, successful entrepreneurs have a plan for their day. *They know that there is no lack of time, there is only a lack of focus and organization.*

Therefore, they develop organization by focusing on their purpose, priorities, and results they are committed to achieving. Then they concentrate on taking the smallest number of activities that will produce these results.

Conscious Millionaires know the #1 secret to creating a millionaire success day. That secret is to develop a daily *purpose*. A purpose not only provides you with a focus for the day, it also ties your day to your longer term goals. It keeps you conscious of how important every action you take and result you achieve is, to your overall business success.

The unfortunate reality is most entrepreneurs have no specific purpose for their day. At most they create a "to-do list" and deal with a lot of fires that need putting out. At the end of the day, half their tasks are still *not finished*. The "to-do list" was their entire plan for the day.

This approach will not only make entrepreneurs more frustrated, overwhelmed, and stressed, it can also result in their team feeling like failures. It seems they keep working harder, but never really make progress. Does this sound familiar? Worse, does it *feel* familiar?

> Conscious Millionaires know the #1 secret to creating a millionaire success day. That secret is to develop a daily purpose.

If you want to maximize the results you achieve daily so you rapidly become a Conscious Millionaire, you can't afford to operate this way. Establish a focused plan for your day. Consciously choose results that excite you so you feel motivated to reach them.

Now, the plan I'm about to share with you will help you become 100 percent results focused. The more you utilize the plan, the more effective and efficient you will become at attaining your results. I developed this several years ago and use it personally; and I teach it to every private client.

Many of my clients say they doubled, tripled, even quadrupled their results the very first week they used the *Conscious Millionaire Daily Plan*™. I look forward to hearing from you and learning how this plan helped you increase your productivity.

These are the components for your *Conscious Millionaire Daily Plan*:

1. Purpose: Develop a clear *purpose* for your day. Your purpose connects your day with one or more of your major business goals. These could include your one-month, quarterly, or one-year goals. If you want to rapidly achieve business success and become financially independent, then each day choose a purpose that moves you toward one of your top business goals. In addition, consider developing a company-wide purpose for each week. This will provide guidance for what you choose as being most important for your business.

2. Standard: Choose one of the three millionaire standards. If you are working on a project that has a hard deadline and is only a few days or weeks into the future, consider challenging yourself by using the "no excuse" standard. Clearly define your standard and hold yourself fully accountable to achieve it.

By using the daily plan,
you will rapidly multiply results.

3. Priorities: Consciously choose one to three priorities for your day. Further, consider your priorities as being 80% of your focus for the day. The other 20% will be various unexpected events and minutia of your day. List your priorities in order of importance. If an emergency occurs or an unexpected event interrupts your day, focus on accomplishing what is under priority one before two, and what is under priority two before three.

 4. Critical Results: Under each priority, list one or more results you identify as being critical for you to achieve today. Your priorities drive your results and your results drive your actions for your day. Develop a specific time for completing each of these critical results. Establishing completion times helps you stay focused and efficient, so you complete your actions and results on time—every time.

5. Why Critical: Each of your results should provide a measurable ROI (return on investment) to your business. Think of ROI is in terms of your traffic, (marketing) sales (revenue), and product/service development and delivery.

6. Focused Actions: These are the *focused actions* that link each priority with a result. Choose the least number of actions necessary to attain your results.

Example of your *Conscious Millionaire Daily Plan:*

Conscious Millionaire Daily Plan

TODAY'S PURPOSE
Move toward your business profit goal

TODAY'S STANDARD
Control Based

PRIORITY 1	PRIORITY 2	PRIORITY 3
Sales Calls	Rally Team	Client Meetings
Focused Actions	**Focused Actions**	**Focused Actions**
Choose 10 prospects	Prepare for meeting	Review client files
Use script to call	Hold team meeting	Lunch meeting client 1
Set up appointments	Engage each member	3 pm meeting client 2
Follow-up emails	Create week's goals	Schedule follow-up
CRITICAL RESULTS	**CRITICAL RESULTS**	**CRITICAL RESULTS**
3 new appointments completed by 3 P.M.	Members have goals completed by 11 A.M.	$5,000 in new orders completed by 6 P.M.
WHY CRITICAL	**WHY CRITICAL**	**WHY CRITICAL**
Fill Revenue Pipeline	Become More Efficient	Grow Revenue / Profits

Note: At the end of each workday, create your plan for the next workday. If you work Monday through Friday, then at the end of Friday, make your plan for Monday. This allows your subconscious to think about your plan. When you start your next workday, review your plan, make any needed adjustments, and begin rapidly putting it into action.

> **Coaching:** Open your *Conscious Millionaire Journal*. Describe how you will utilize the *Conscious Millionaire Daily Plan* over the next three days. Enter comments on what you learned and how much more productive you became by using the *Plan* each day.

Consciously Create Your Day

Consciously set up your day for millionaire success. Whenever you start your day—morning, afternoon, or evening—use these three keys to consciously create your day:

1. Clear and Focus Your Mind: Bring yourself into a state of mindful awareness by focusing on your breath for five to fifteen minutes. This is a basic form of breath meditation. Sit in a chair with your feet flat on the floor or sit on the floor. Consider using a meditation cushion. Place your hands on your lap with your palms facing up and your fingers overlapping. Hold your spine erect and put your tongue on the roof of your mouth. Then lower your gaze so that your eyes are at a 45 degree angle with the floor. "Soften" your eyes so they slightly defocus.

Put your attention on your breath as you allow yourself to slowly breathe out and then gently breathe back into your body. If you become distracted by your thoughts or anything else, simply bring your attention back to your breath. Breath meditation not only centers and grounds you; it also opens more space in your mind so you have room for new ideas throughout your day. Think of your meditation as practicing being present.

> Breath meditation not only *centers* and *grounds* you; it also opens more space in your mind.

2. Review Your *Conscious Millionaire Daily Plan*: Once your mind is clear, take out your one-page plan that you created at the end of the previous workday. Review your purpose, standard, one to three priorities, and desired results. Then read through your actions and targeted times for completing each result. Make any adjustments you feel are needed so you have a realistic plan you can accomplish at the millionaire standard you chose. The *less* you focus on, generally the *more* you achieve.

3. Visualize Your Success: Now that you have a clear plan for your work day, it's time to use *Conscious Millionaire Visualization*. Do this in the morning; visualize what you will achieve *today*. Consciously envision easily achieving all of your results by the end of your day. See, hear, physically sense, taste, smell, and emotionally feel what your success will be like. Focus your mind and heart on the results you will achieve today. See these results moving toward you, and then coming into your body.

Then, prepare to take action by rehearsing your day in your mind. As you do, see yourself taking your planned actions. As you see them in your mind, begin taking the actions you outlined in your daily plan. Develop momentum by taking *three* to *five* easy success actions now. Review the "Conscious Millionaire Visualization" section found at the end of Chapter 2, *Formula for Creating Wealth*.

> **Coaching:** Open your *Conscious Millionaire Journal*. Write the following statement and fill in the blank. Then say it out loud three times. "Today, I am committed to achieving_____, _____, and _____." (Fill in one result for each of your three priorities for today.)

End of Your Day: Revitalize and Refocus

Complete your millionaire success day by allowing time to relax, rest, and restore yourself so you are ready to achieve another millionaire success day tomorrow. Your three focused actions for achieving this are:

1. Revitalize: Allow time to relax from your day and revitalize yourself. Although you may have specific business, financial, or educational work to carry out after your normal workday, instead of filling your evenings with mechanically *doing*, allow time for *being*. Turn off the television and spend quality time with yourself, friends, and family. If you want to achieve maximum vitality and create more success tomorrow, allow time each day to revitalize your mind, heart, body, and spirit.

2. Prepare for Rest: You will have much more energy tomorrow, if you *prepare* for *quality rest* today. Finish eating and drinking any alcohol or caffeine drinks at least two to three hours before bed. An hour before you go to bed, stop stimulating yourself with television, phone calls, detail work, the Internet, or information-packed reading. Allow your mind, body, emotions, and spirit to *slow down before* you get into bed. You will sleep much more deeply and wake up more rested.

3. Focus Your Mind: Finish your day by focusing your mind on success. Just before bed, ask yourself one question; this instructs the unconscious aspects of your mind to focus on answering it while you sleep. *For example*: Ask for the solution to a business problem, how to achieve a specific result, or an action that would help grow your business. When you wake in the morning, you will often have an answer. Keep a notepad by your bed to record your nightly questions and morning answers.

Conscious Focused Action Model

This is the fifth version of the foundational model, which is found in Chapter 2, *Formula for Creating Wealth*.

The conscious level and focus level interrelate by utilizing each of the words on the conscious level with the focal points on the two tiers of the focus level. *For example*: Utilizing "purpose" from the focus level, ask:

• "What result will our business *purpose* help achieve?" and, "Why is using our business *purpose* to accomplish this result a priority?"

• "Who will benefit from using the *purpose* to achieve this result?" and, "Who will help use the *purpose* to attain this result?"

CONSCIOUS FOCUSED ACTION MODEL - 5

- "How can I best utilize the *purpose* to reach this result?"

Approach the other three levels—action, result, and learning—the same as in the foundational model. If you don't fully achieve your desired result, want to improve your process, or care to achieve your result at a higher level, then iterate. Review each level to determine what needs to change. Return to the conscious level and make the changes as you go through the model again. Then *test* the changes to determine if they are actually better.

CONSCIOUS MILLIONAIRE COACHING

Build Your Strategy

Open your *Conscious Millionaire Journal.* Write a three-step business strategy using *conscious focused action.* Develop your strategy utilizing the concept provided in the *conscious* step below. It is an important concept from this chapter.

1. Conscious: Consider the importance of having a company-wide purpose for each week. Create a goal of developing and communicating it to your staff, even if your staff is one virtual assistant. *For example*: "At the end of each week select a business purpose for the next week based upon what you most want to achieve and communicate it to everyone in your company via email."

2. Focused: As you focus on your goal, choose three actions that will help you begin to achieve it. Determine the precise order for your actions.

3. Action: During the next twenty-four hours, execute by taking your three actions.

Grow Your Business

In your *Conscious Millionaire Journal* make notes on how you utilize each of the following to grow your business:

• Select one of the millionaire standards; then use it to measure all of your business results this week.

• Implement the *Conscious Millionaire Daily Plan* as a "master plan" for your team. Then assign different results and actions to various team members.

• Identify at least three distractions that tend to get you off track. Eliminate each of them and notice how much more productive you become.

Create Your Journey

Here are three choices for what to read next. The first is to read another *conscious* section. The second is to read another *millionaire* section. The third choice is to *journey* through the book linearly, reading it chapter by chapter.

 Conscious: Consider reading the "Develop A Growth Culture" section in Chapter 13, *Prepare for Fast Growth*, before continuing to the next chapter.

 Millionaire: Take a look at the "Conscious Money Habits" section in Chapter 11, *Achieve Financial Freedom*, before going to the next chapter.

 Journey: Continue forward to Chapter 7, *Your Millionaire Inner Zone*.

QR Codes / Links

 Go to the membership site to view a coaching video that reveals how to best utilize the *Conscious Millionaire Daily Plan*. While there, download a free worksheet for you and your team to use in creating your daily plan. Access the site now at:

ConsciousMillionaire.com/member

YOUR MILLIONAIRE INNER ZONE

Trust perfect timing.

In the previous chapter, you learned how to become more productive primarily by utilizing logical skills, such as prioritizing. In this chapter, you learn how to access more of your right brain abilities to produce results with *effortless speed and ease*. You will also discover the two dimensions of your *Millionaire Inner Zone*™, which are flow and focus. You'll understand the power of synchronicity and how to utilize intuition. Also, you will learn how to achieve perfect timing in your business and life. Then you will utilize the *Conscious Focused Action Model* to move forward on your Conscious Millionaire Journey.

WEALTH WITH SPEED AND EASE

Do you remember a time in your life when everything began to unfold with astonishing speed? When the answers, people, and resources you needed all just seemed to naturally flow into your business and personal life? You knew what decisions to make and which actions to take, almost instinctively. Everything moved forward almost effortlessly. This is what it is like when you are in your *Millionaire Inner Zone*.

Imagine a day at your office in which everything unfolds rapidly and in a way that feels almost effortless. Your stress melts away. Obstacles disappear. Your insights are on target. You feel in harmony with the world and environment around you. Both you and your business appear to be in the right place, at the right time, doing the right thing.

When you enter your *Millionaire Inner Zone*, you experience a heightened state of awareness and competency. You feel like you are in the flow of life, effortlessly moving forward with speed and ease.

Now, what if you could create this type of day whenever you want? What if instead of feeling that your business is a day-to-day struggle, filled with massive stress, hassles, and constant worries that you could go under, you learn to enter your *Millionaire InnerZone*. As a result, you attract into your life the resources, customers, and opportunities you need to make your business thrive—with effortless speed and ease.

> When you enter your *Millionaire Inner Zone,* you experience a heightened state of awareness and competency.

How much faster would you grow your business? How many more customers, sales, and profits would you generate? How much more would you enjoy your life and business? How quickly would you shift from surviving to thriving? How much more alive would you feel?

How much more excited would you be about growing your business? How much more emotionally invested in your future would you become?

When you enter this zone, you are in a powerful *state*. Think of state as the sum total of how you are being at any moment; how you are *thinking, feeling*, and *acting*.

The *Millionaire Inner Zone* is a state in which your *energy* moves faster and you feel *more connected* to all the energy that is around you. You are literally more conscious and awake.

When athletes perform at their best, they talk about being "in the zone." They gain access to a heightened state of awareness and competency by entering the zone. Their senses and response patterns become super activated. When you enter your *Millionaire Inner Zone*, you can have the same experience.

People who achieve at their highest level both live and conduct business in their zone. For them, it is a *way of life*. This is the path to wealth that is easier and faster. Why? Because when you are in your zone, you are moving with the flow of life, instead of against it.

> *Your Millionaire Inner Zone*
> *is a state of peak performance!*

Because you are more conscious and connected when you are in your zone, you take in more information and notice more opportunities. You have precise intuition and hunches available to you. As a result, you tend to grow your business faster, make better investment decisions, and make more money. Moving into a higher energy state, you begin to tap into your visionary consciousness. When you connect to energy at this level, you naturally create a broader vision of what is possible, not only for yourself, but for others and the world. You envision innovative products, new services, and creative ways to solve your customers' problems. It's as if you know what your customers will want and need even before they do.

When you are in your *Millionaire Inner Zone*, you begin to trust your experiences and intuition, rather than constantly second-guessing yourself. When you are in your zone, you feel that you are on-path. Your business and financial results confirm that you are headed in the right direction.

THE TWO DIMENSIONS OF ZONE

There are two dimensions to *Millionaire Inner Zone*. The first dimension is *flow-zone*; the second dimension is *focus-zone*. By combining the power of flow and focus, you not only achieve your overall results faster and easier, you target specific results and then achieve them at warp speed.

Think of *flow* as the foundational dimension of zone. It represents how you want to live and conduct your business on a daily basis. It is the state in which you increase the speed at which you move your company forward. When you are in flow, you reach your desired result by taking a path that feels authentic and right for you. Moreover, your actions are fully aligned with the direction in which your life is naturally headed.

Next consider the *focus* dimension of zone. You enter this dimension when you want to achieve a *specific result quickly*. You accomplish this by becoming laser focused on your desired result. This is what athletes usually mean when they talk about getting in the zone.

They become totally focused, and feel a sense of oneness with their goal, as if they had already achieved it. *For example*: They catch the pass, sink the basketball, or make the putt.

Athletes who credit being in this *focus-zone* for achieving their best, include basketball superstar Michael Jordan, Olympic Gold speed skater Apollo Ohno, and Olympic Gold swimmer Michael Phelps. They all talk about instinctively knowing what to do when they are deep in this focused dimension of flow.

By spending time in your *Millionaire Inner Zone*, you will learn to instinctively know what to do next.

YOUR FIRST DIMENSION: FLOW-ZONE

There are three keys to entering your *flow-zone*. I discovered them over a seven-year period after selling our family companies. I traveled, lived in different places, and noticed that some days everything just naturally came together. I met the right people, found the resources I required, and received the answers I needed. I achieved my results in a nearly effortlessly way.

Because of my studies in pre-medicine and my interest in the sciences, I take a scientific approach to achieving optimum performance. This includes understanding how to duplicate peak states. So, I naturally became curious as to why some days everything seemed to *flow* effortlessly, and other days nothing seemed to go right.

I began to keep notes. I looked for commonalities between the days when the right decisions came to me easily and naturally, and the days when they didn't. I wanted to learn how to create flow anytime, and anywhere, I chose.

I discovered there were precisely three things I did on the days when I was in flow that I wasn't doing on the other days. I began to experiment by intentionally choosing to do these things. When I did, I immediately started to experience *flow*.

Curious as to whether other people would have the same result, I began to teach these steps to friends. Their results were similar to mine. Whenever they used the three keys, they too experienced flow.

Later, I began teaching the keys to clients. I found it significantly increased the speed in which they could achieve business goals, connect with the right opportunities, and move forward with a deeper sense of harmony. The three keys are:

1. Be Present: Think, feel, and act with present awareness; be in the here and now. Flow doesn't occur in the past or the future. Flow only occurs in the present, in the now. It is only when you are present in the moment that you connect to the life energy flowing all around you. One way to become present is to focus on your breath. As you slowly breathe in and out three times, notice how you feel present and grounded.

2. Be Open: Discard preconceived ideas about your life, or how specifically you will achieve your goals. Be open to discovering new ways of achieving what you want. Be willing for life and business to unfold in ways you may not have expected. One way to become more open is to imagine there are 100 possibilities for how to achieve any goal. By noticing how events naturally come together, the right steps will become obvious to you.

3. Be Authentic: Connect to a place within yourself that feels real and genuine. Notice what resonates with you as being true. Each of us has an instinct to know if we are on the right path and are taking the right actions for us. Some people have a sensation somewhere in their body, such as a gut feeling; others hear a specific sound or tone inside themselves; while other people see an answer as if it were written in their mind. Notice how this occurs for you, and then experiment with flow in your life and business. Think of this as a new adventure.

Coaching: Open your *Conscious Millionaire Journal*. For the next three days, practice being in your *flow-zone* by becoming present, open, and authentic. At the completion of each day, in your journal describe your experiences and the results you achieved.

Your Second Dimension: Focus-Zone

When you want to achieve a *specific result at warp speed*, move into the focused dimension of your *Millionaire Inner Zone*. When you create laser focus, you are in your optimal state of mental, emotional, and psychological performance. You are in a state of maximum productivity and personal competency.

You possess total clarity of the result you want and develop a strong desire to rapidly achieve it. You become optimistic and self-confident that you *will* attain your result. As you clear your mind of distracting thoughts and eliminate negative beliefs and feelings, you develop a *focused* state that gives you an extra edge.

Your *Millionaire Inner Zone* is a powerful energy state in which you are so laser focused on your outcome that you begin to experience *you and your desired result* as being ONE. Moreover, as your energy state begins to resonate with the result you want, you also begin to attract the people, resources, and opportunities that will help achieve your result.

> *You achieve results rapidly*
> *in your Millionaire Inner Zone.*

When you are in this laser-focused dimension of zone, you often experience a slowing down of time. This is because you become so fully present and focused on your activities that you lose all sense of past, present, and future.

However, the moment you look up at the clock, you realize you've been so absorbed in your concentration that you've actually been focused for hours, instead of minutes.

The seven keys to achieving results rapidly in your *focus-zone* are:

1. Deeply relax and connect to your *flow-zone*.

2. Clearly define one specific result you desire to achieve.

3. Concentrate on your result and feel committed to achieving it.

4. Laser focus your mind by focusing your thoughts on your result.

5. Laser focus your emotions; put your whole heart into your result.

6. Laser focus your actions by taking one *conscious focused action* after another so you move relentlessly toward your desired result.

7. Feel a confident optimism as you begin to experience a sense of oneness with the result you desire. This is the same type of *oneness* you develop when you use *Conscious Millionaire Visualization*. See the future move into the present. Experience your goal as being one with the present moment.

As you perform each of these steps, put your full energy into achieving your desired result. As you become *laser-focused*, *confident*, and *relaxed*, you will naturally enter a state in which you achieve goals faster. This state is your *focus-zone*.

> **Coaching:** Open your *Conscious Millionaire Journal*. Identify one result that you can achieve by being in your *focus-zone*. Write the desired result in your journal. Then utilize the seven steps outlined in this section to attain your result. Describe your experience.

The Power of Synchronicity

Have you ever thought of telephoning someone, only to have them call at that moment? Have you had a question in mind, randomly opened a book and discovered the answer? Or, have you ever needed a specific amount of money and just that amount appeared unexpectedly? Perhaps it came in the form of a business opportunity, unanticipated sale, or past due client who sent a check.

This is the experience of synchronicity. It happens when events come together in unexpected ways that represent a personal meaning to you. Synchronicity is the natural result of living in flow and is a powerful tool that can help you grow your business.

> The more you live and do business in your *flow-zone*, the more frequently you will experience synchronicity.

You turn on the television and notice an advertisement for a business conference in your home town. It feels right, so you attend, only to meet several people with whom you ultimately do business. You look for new customers and are unexpectedly invited to speak to a group. As a result, you gain several new customers.

The more you live and conduct business in your *flow-zone*, the more frequently you will experience synchronicity. This is because synchronicity results from being in flow.

As you experience synchronicity, the people, money, and opportunities you need will begin to enter your life. The resources you need for a business project will materialize at the time you need them. And the answers you seek will naturally come into your life through a phone call, something you read, or maybe an impromptu conversation with someone you bump into on the street.

When you are in your *Millionaire Inner Zone*, synchronicity naturally occurs. How much faster and easier would you become a Conscious Millionaire by tapping into the amazing power of synchronicity?

> **Coaching:** Open your *Conscious Millionaire Journal*. For the next three days, record all the synchronous occurrences you experience each day. Include how you chose to utilize them to grow your business or live more fully.

Develop Your Intuitive Edge

Recall the discussion of physics in the "Science of Conscious Success" section at the beginning of Chapter 3, *Win by Becoming Conscious*. It's a law of physics that everything is energy. You are energy. Your body, thoughts, and emotions are energy. Art and music are energy. This book is energy. Everything around you is energy. All of life is an interconnected web of energy.

Embedded in this energy is pure intelligence. When you enter your *Millionaire Inner Zone*, you create a heightened sense of awareness that helps you become conscious of this information.

There are two aspects to your intuition. The first aspect is becoming aware of the information embedded in the energy that is flowing through you. *For example*: Noticing your hunches and intuitive insights throughout your day.

> You learn to trust your intuitive insights one experience and one result at a time

The second aspect of intuition results from comparing your awareness of your current situation with your lifetime of experiences. *For example*: Because of your expert experience in a specific area, you may only need a few pieces of data in order to identify a trend as it is beginning to emerge. By combining both aspects of intuition, you develop more accurate insights.

Take this a step further and you have what I call *whole brain intuition*. It becomes whole brain by combining logic (left brain) and intuition (right brain). When you utilize both sides of your brain, you have a more complete insight as to what to do next.

This is because the logical and intuitive parts of your mind are working together to create an even more robust insight. This allows for a split-second sense of *what actions* to take, in *which order*, and *when*.

Now, ask yourself how much larger would you grow your business if you developed your intuitive edge and began using it as your personal *money making secret*. How many more customers would you acquire? How many more opportunities would you notice? How much faster would you increase your revenue?

By spending time in your *Millionaire Inner Zone*, you build trust in your intuition in the same way you build trust with a friend or business associate. You learn to trust your intuitive insights one experience and one result at a time.

I use my intuitive hunches and insights in making my financial decisions. So does every successful business person and investor I know. And, so can you.

If you want to make better business decisions, grow your business and profits faster, and achieve lasting financial freedom, then hone your intuitive skills.

Everyone experiences intuition at times. It may come in the form of a gut hunch, an urging to make one decision over another, or the sense to take a right turn instead of a left. Sometimes you are highly conscious of your intuition. It is a clear, definite feeling. It is unequivocal. At other times, you sense something that seems like it is just outside of your awareness.

You have an "inkling," which is a great word that means allowing ideas and insights to emerge from deep within. Inkling is often the beginning stage of developing intuition.

Likewise, when you first learned of *Conscious Millionaire*, you may have had an intuition that it contains information that will help you make more money. You may have also sensed that it would show you how to turn the difference you want to make into a profitable business.

You may have felt it would reveal a path to business success and wealth that would be right for you, one that would help you thrive. As a result, you are reading it now.

The more connected you become in your *Millionaire Inner Zone*, the more you will pick up information in the form of intuition. How?

When you are in your zone, you become more in tune with what is occurring each present moment. You also are more aware of the direction in which *energy* is flowing. This helps you notice where your life, business, and even opportunities are headed.

One of the best ways to fine-tune your awareness and develop your intuition is to pay attention to what you are sensing—seeing, hearing, physically sensing, tasting, and smelling—when your intuition is accurate.

> When you are in your zone, you become more in tune with what is occurring each present moment.

Do you *visualize* a specific picture or see words and numbers in your mind? Do you *hear* a particular inner sound, voice, or words inside your head? Do you experience a physical *sensation*, such as a tingling or pressure, in some area of your body? Are there particular *tastes* or *smells* that occur when your intuition is accurate?

Think of your senses as your physical *markers* for when your intuition is accurate. Over time, you will develop an understanding of when to *trust* and *act* upon your intuitions. As you fine-tune your intuition, utilize it to help you become a Conscious Millionaire.

Coaching: Open your *Conscious Millionaire Journal*. Keep track of the visual, auditory, and physical sensations that occur when your intuition is spot-on accurate. What is the order in which they occur? Notice if they form a pattern.

Connect with Perfect Timing

In this chapter, you learned how to enter your *Millionaire Inner Zone* to achieve wealth with greater speed and ease. Specifically, you discovered how to access both your *flow-zone* and *focus-zone*.

You also learned how to utilize your intuition, including what it means to use whole brain intuition. You discovered the power of synchronicity, the experience of unexpected events coming together in a way that is personally meaningful for you.

Now it's time to develop an even deeper understanding of the *Millionaire Inner Zone*. Based upon what you learned within this chapter, together with the information contained in Chapter 3, *Win by Becoming Conscious*, you already know that everything in our universe is intelligent energy. It flows around you and through you at all times.

Think of yourself as being part of a larger energy mosaic, one in which all the energy in the universe is interconnected in meaningful ways.

Open your consciousness even further and imagine that all the life energy in the universe is moving together in one *purposeful direction*. It is purposeful because it is an expression of a larger plan, one in which you and I are here to play a role. How we play that role is always our choice.

View the energy that comprises this plan as being alive, unfolding, and constantly evolving. Further consider the possibility that everything occurs with perfect timing.

It is only because everything in your *flow-zone* is occurring with perfect timing, that synchronicity is possible. At the precise moment you *become present*, *open*, and *authentic*, you connect with this perfect timing in a way that is right for you. It is also right for all those with whom you come in contact. Flow is your authentic path forward.

As you go deeper into flow and begin to act in harmony with it, perfect timing is revealed through a myriad of synchronous events that begin to occur in your life and business. It also expresses through the urgings, insights, and hunches within you.

Many people report feeling as if they are being guided. Sometimes this "guidance" occurs gently. At other times, if feels more like a truck just hit them. However it occurs, they feel the information that is revealed, including which steps to take next, is being provided at the perfect time.

Think of connecting to your *flow-zone* as a practice, one that leads to your learning how to access perfect timing. The more you practice being present, open, and authentic, the more skilled you will become at noticing how perfect timing is occurring in your life and business.

As you start to live in your *Millionaire Inner Zone*, you will begin to sense that everything is occurring within a bigger matrix of perfect timing. You will experience your life and business as being on the path that feels right to you.

This perspective leads to a profound understanding of how your life and business unfolds when you choose to be in the *flow-zone*. As you connect to the energetic web of life that exists all around you, a natural timing seems to occur, one that you can bring into your life and business. You may have had this experience before. Recall what it felt like.

> *There is a perfect timing*
> *that is occurring all around you.*

I consider this material so important in creating wealth and success, that many years ago I chose *trust perfect timing* as my personal motto. What this motto means to me is that when I enter flow, everything in my life and business occurs with a sense of perfect timing.

While my ego may want things to happen in a different order or manner, I've learned to trust that when I am present, open, and authentic, that I will obtain a deeper knowing about which actions to take and when. Furthermore, these actions appear to not only be in my best interest, but in the best interest of all those my actions touch.

For some people, *perfect timing* is profoundly spiritual in nature. Many report that the more they live in harmony with this flowing energy field that surrounds them, the more they feel joyful, fulfilled, and spiritually connected with all of life. Have you ever had this experience?

Spiritual experiences often deepen the moment one develops

> Enter the *Millionaire Inner Zone* and become a master of perfect timing.

a consciousness that we are each part of something bigger, a larger plan. While our minds may not be able to logically comprehend the vastness of this profound reality, this plan seems to be unfolding with perfect timing.

While each of us may have our own understanding of how this bigger plan and timing work, it appears to be dynamic and constantly evolving. This purposeful direction seems to both respond to the needs of the world and be influenced by the *consciousness* that you and I express at any given moment.

In this sense, we are each part of the evolution of a bigger plan. You connect with this larger *perfect timing* when you are in your *flow-zone*, doing what feels authentic for you.

It seems unlikely that any entrepreneur or investor could ever reach their full potential, make their biggest difference, or achieve their greatest wealth without learning to connect with perfect timing. Just as many of my clients have developed this skill, you can as well. By applying the material in this chapter, you can learn how to enter the *Millionaire Inner Zone* and become a master of perfect timing.

CONSCIOUS FOCUSED ACTION MODEL

In this chapter are versions six and seven of the model. The sixth version is utilized for *flow-zone*, and the seventh version is utilized for *focus-zone*. Let's address the flow-zone version of the model first.

This model is different at the conscious level by including the three keys to entering your *flow-zone*: *present*, *open*, and *authentic*. It is also different at the action level by including *whole brain intuition*.

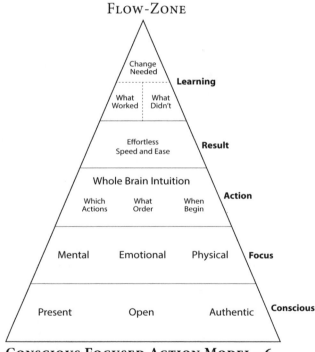

FLOW-ZONE

CONSCIOUS FOCUSED ACTION MODEL - 6

The conscious level of this model consists of the three keys to entering your *flow-zone*: *present*, *open*, and *authentic*. Think of these three keys as working together as a whole to create a *flow-zone state*. The focus level is the same as in the foundational model: *mental*, *emotional*, and *physical*.

The action level contains two tiers. The top tier is *whole brain intuition*, which allows for split-second decisions. The bottom tier contains the action decisions: *which actions, what order*, and *when to begin*.

The result level changes to one desired result: *effortless speed and ease*. When you are in your *flow-zone*, you do not focus on a specific external result. Instead, you focus on how to best achieve a state of effortless speed and ease.

Approach the learning level the same as the foundational model. If you didn't fully achieve your desired result, which is moving forward with *effortless speed and ease*, then iterate. Determine what needs to change. Return to the conscious level and make the changes as you go through the model again.

FOCUS-ZONE

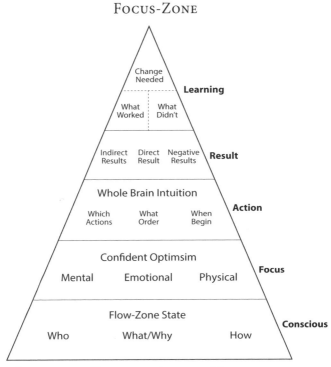

CONSCIOUS FOCUSED ACTION MODEL - 7

Now, let's address the seventh version of the model which is *focus-zone*. It is different at the conscious level by beginning in a *flow-zone* state. It is also different at the action level by including *whole brain intuition*.

In this version of the model, the *conscious* level has two interrelated tiers. The top tier is the *flow-zone state*. The bottom tier is the same as in the foundational model: *who, what/why,* and *how*. While in the flow-zone state, ask each of the bottom tier questions. *For example*:

- "What result do I want to achieve?" and, "Why is achieving this result a priority?"

- "Who will benefit from my achieving this result?" and, "Who will help me attain this result?"

- "How can I best reach this result?"

The focus level is the same as in the foundational model. However, in this model, approach each aspect—mental, emotional, and physical—with a confident optimism.

The action level is identical to the *flow-zone* version of the model: the top tier is whole brain intuition. The bottom tier contains the action decisions: *which actions, what order, when to begin*. Utilize your whole brain intuition to make each of your action decisions.

Approach the other two levels—result and learning—the same as in the foundational model. If you don't fully achieve your desired result, want to improve your process, or care to achieve your result at a higher level, then iterate. Review each level to determine what needs to change. Return to the conscious level and make the changes as you go through the model again. Then *test* the changes to determine if they are actually better.

CONSCIOUS MILLIONAIRE COACHING

Build Your Strategy

Open your *Conscious Millionaire Journal*. Write a three-step business strategy using *conscious focused action*. Develop your strategy utilizing the concept provided in the *conscious* step below. It is an important concept from this chapter.

1. Conscious: Develop a goal of being in your *flow-zone* when you make business decisions. *For example*: "I begin each business day by being in *flow-zone*, then make decisions that feel authentic and right to me."

2. Focused: As you focus on your goal, choose three actions that will help you begin to achieve it. Determine the precise order for your actions.

3. Action: During the next twenty-four hours, execute by taking your three actions.

Grow Your Business

In your *Conscious Millionaire Journal* make notes on how you utilize each of the following to grow your business:

• Share the information about how to enter flow with your team. Make it a part of your culture and how you conduct business.

• Select a goal for your business and become laser focused in the *Millionaire Inner Zone* to rapidly achieve it.

• Utilize your intuition to help make your business decisions this week. Keep track of how many times you are accurate. How much more money did you make using your intuition?

Create Your Journey

Here are three choices for what to read next. The first is to read another *conscious* section. The second is to read another *millionaire* section. The third choice is to *journey* through the book linearly, reading it chapter by chapter. continued

Conscious: You may want to review the "Science of Conscious Success" section in Chapter 3, *Win by Becoming Conscious*, before continuing to the next chapter.

 Millionaire: Take a look at the "Conscious Millionaire Motivation" section in Chapter 14, *Create Your Millionaire Plan*, before going to the next chapter.

 Journey: Continue forward to Chapter 8, *Create an Abundance Mindset*.

QR Codes / Links

 Go to the membership site to listen to an audio that guides you into your own *flow-zone* experience. Access the site now at:

ConsciousMillionaire.com/ member

CREATE
AN ABUNDANCE
MINDSET

*Entrepreneurs with abundance mindsets
create the highest levels of wealth!*

In this chapter, you discover the importance of shifting from scarcity to abundance thinking. You will learn how your beliefs filter what you see and believe you can accomplish. Then you will understand the "money-purpose wound" and how to turn *limiting* money beliefs into *empowering* beliefs. You will also discover how to develop the mindset of a highly-successful entrepreneur as you discover more secrets for growing businesses. Lastly, you will utilize the *Conscious Focused Action Model* to move forward on your Conscious Millionaire Journey.

SHIFT FROM SCARCITY TO ABUNDANCE

Unfortunately, instead of easily making profits and becoming successful, many entrepreneurs remain stuck in a scarcity mindset. This is a mindset of *lack*—a set of beliefs that there *isn't enough*: time, resources, customers, talent, opportunities, or money to go around.

When entrepreneurs buy into these scarcity beliefs, they often begin to struggle, feel frustrated, and start telling themselves they are worthless, that they will never accomplish much with their lives.

They may beat themselves up emotionally and feel like giving up. Scarcity thinking can even result in feeling like a victim instead of being in charge of your life and business. Have you ever felt this way?

Business owners trapped in a scarcity outlook sometimes think they must destroy their competition, literally crush them and put them out of business, just to make ends meet and pay bills. At times, they may even violate their own values by resorting to lying or cheating, when they actually desire to be honest and fair with others.

They don't act in these ways because they are bad people. Because they are afraid they will fail miserably, they act in ways they normally wouldn't. This fear is fueled in part by their mindset of "lack." It is also fueled by their sense of *separateness*.

> Your scarcity beliefs literally block you from seeing the abundant opportunities all around you.

Because they believe they are separate from others, instead of being part of a larger whole, they feel compelled to try to win by taking what they perceive as being *scarce* resources from others.

When your mind is filled with scarcity thoughts, it's difficult, if not impossible, to consistently be in your *Millionaire Inner Zone*. Therefore, rather than moving with the abundant flow of life, your scarcity actions actually result in your moving against it.

With a negative reality inside your mind, your own beliefs and inner chatter act against you, rather than in your best interest. Your scarcity beliefs literally block you from seeing the abundant opportunities all around you.

One of the most prevalent scarcity thoughts is "wealth is a zero-sum game." When you think of wealth in this way, you falsely believe that for you to win, someone else must lose.

Why?

Because you tell yourself there is a *finite* amount of wealth in the world, you think you must grab "your share" before someone else takes it. Have you ever found yourself thinking in this way?

Unfortunately, deep down in the recesses of your unconscious mind, I guarantee that beliefs like this are hovering in some dark corner. Why do I say this? Because the prevalent view today is there is a finite amount of wealth, so there is never enough to go around. It is imbedded in our cultural mindset.

We are taught in school and business trainings to outcompete other businesses for scarce resources, which includes customers. It's communicated repeatedly on financial networks. This viewpoint is found in business books, magazines, and newspapers. Without even realizing it, you have probably been affected by this way of thinking.

If you want to do a large amount of good in the world, grow your business, and enjoy a life of true abundance, then you can not afford to allow scarcity thinking to cripple your chances. Bring every scarcity thought that is within you into the light of day, examine it, and then discard it as being false!

The first belief to discard is the very idea there is a fixed amount of wealth in the world. Why? Because essentially this is the root of scarcity thinking. If there were actually a fixed amount of wealth, then in a world in which the population is expanding, there would not be enough wealth to go around. However, this belief is 100 percent false.

Think about this belief carefully and it will become immediately clear why it is false. If there was a fixed amount of wealth in the world, then there would always be the same level of wealth every day, of every week, of every year. It would never vary.

However, that doesn't appear to be the case. The actual total amount of wealth in the world is a dynamic quantity—it's constantly changing.

There are periods of economic expansion and periods of economic contraction, or recessions. Stock markets and asset values, like home prices, go up and down. However, the most important news is that wealth, when viewed over a period of decades and centuries, is always expanding. How does this occur?

The answer is found in how you create wealth. You create wealth by adding value to other people, businesses, organizations, and society. In exchange for the value you add, wealth is returned to you, usually in the form of financial payment.

> You produce greater value in the marketplace by *collaborating* with one another.

There is no limit to the amount of wealth that you, I, and the other billions of people on this planet can add to one another. That's true, isn't it? Absolutely. This is why wealth is infinitely expansive.

You produce greater value in the marketplace by *collaborating* with one another. When two or more people come together with the stated intention of each benefiting, they produce new synergies and ideas for how to add value to customers.

This is why collaborating with other firms in your field produces more ways to add value to the marketplace and, therefore, more ways for each of you to create wealth.

Furthermore, not only is the population expanding over time, far more importantly, the technologies for collaborating and discovering new ways to add value are also exponentially expanding. Every year the methods, means, and avenues for providing value to your customers increase.

As they grow, more opportunities to create wealth automatically appear. Therefore, the amount of value that we can add collectively is expanding rapidly—and with it, our ability to create wealth.

Wealth results from adding value
to others and receiving value in return!

Ponder these questions for a moment: Is there any limit to the ways your business can leverage your relationships and technology to create wealth? Is there any limit to the ways you can market and sell your products? Is there any limit to the amount of value your business can provide to others? Absolutely not!

There is absolutely no limit on how much value your business can deliver and how much wealth you can create. This is why there is no real limit on how much money you can make as an entrepreneur. The same is true for all the other entrepreneurs and businesses in the world.

Because you now realize the old scarcity view of money and wealth is simply inaccurate, you can consciously choose to let go of it—right now. We live in an abundant world, one on limitless wealth potential. There are infinite ways you can create wealth by bringing value to others. The truth is you can create as much wealth as you desire.

This is what it means to enjoy an inspired life as a Conscious Millionaire. It is being in the field of absolute abundance, not as a theory, but as your day to day reality.

Your Beliefs are Filters

A belief is any thought you have repeated so many times that you now regard it as truth. One way you form your beliefs is through the ideas to which you are repeatedly exposed. Another way is by repeating the same thoughts over and over. What are thoughts? They are how you view yourself and your environment. They are your interpretations of reality.

Your beliefs are the filters through which you view life. They determine what you think is possible, where you naturally direct your attention, and how you interpret your life. They also influence which opportunities you see. Your beliefs can either *limit* or *empower* you. How does that occur?

Your mind is comprised of neural networks. Each belief you form creates a specific neural pathway, a neural pattern in your mind. Your mind works by looking for matches. So, if you have an established neural pattern for something, your mind will search for a match in your environment. If it finds one, you will naturally perceive it as being real.

If you don't have an established neural pathway, you lack an established filter for interpreting external reality. Think of a baby and how surprised they are by new experiences. There is no correlation between their internal neural patterns and the new external events. However, as their mind develops neural patterns, they learn to match external events with the patterns. This is also how they develop their beliefs about the world.

So, what happens if you believe that something is *not* possible, like you can *not* make $100,000 profit in a month? You will negate seeing any opportunities to achieve this. It's unlikely you would even attempt to make the money. You would not develop strategies or even take one single action in the hope of attaining the result.

> *Conscious Millionaires understand*
> *that their beliefs influence their results.*

This is because you have an established neural pattern—a belief that opportunities for making this much money don't even exist—*for you*. Even though you may have witnessed others achieve similar results (make this amount of money) and are staring at an opportunity for achieving $100,000 profit this month, you literally don't see the possibility!

And, unfortunately, even if you did "see" the opportunity, because of your limiting belief, you would likely tell yourself that you couldn't use the opportunity to make money. Because you believe it wouldn't work for you! Do you recall a time in which this happened in your life?

For example: If you believe you *can* make a sale to people you meet at networking events, then networking events become great opportunities for you. Because of your belief's established neural pattern, you walk in the room thinking you can make sales. Your mental belief—your mind— empowers you to act on the opportunity and close the sale!

By contrast, if you believe you can *not* make a sale by giving speeches, you limit yourself by your own belief. Your belief neural pattern negates you from speaking as a way to make sales. As long as you maintain this limiting belief, instead of changing it into an empowering belief, public speaking will not be a good opportunity for you to close sales.

> By *consciously choosing* abundance thoughts, you open the door to making a bigger difference and creating bigger profits.

Let's relate beliefs to mindset *and* results. Your beliefs form your mindset. Thus, your mindset influences your behaviors—which lead to your results. When you allow your beliefs, mindset, and behaviors to run your life, without consciously choosing and taking responsibility for each of them, your results are far less gratifying than you truly desire.

Fortunately, your beliefs are thoughts, and thoughts can be changed. You know this by how many times you have already changed your thoughts today. In the time it will take you to read this chapter, you will probably change many of your old thoughts about money and replace them with new thoughts of abundance. By repeatedly thinking these abundance thoughts you will develop new abundance beliefs.

By *consciously choosing* abundance thoughts, you open the door to making a bigger difference and creating bigger profits.

> **Coaching:** Open your *Conscious Millionaire Journal*. Write the following two belief filters: "I can *easily* achieve my goals" and, "These goals are too *difficult* for me." Then under each filter, make a list of results you believe you could accomplish in a single day. Which list inspires you the most?

MONEY-PURPOSE WOUND

In Chapter 4, *Passion, Purpose and Values*, we defined true north as the combination of your passion, purpose and strengths. Unfortunately, some amazingly talented and good-hearted people erroneously think they should not charge when they use their passion, purpose, and strengths to help others.

They reason that "God," a "Higher Power," or the "Universe" gave these to them for free. Therefore, they should only utilize them to provide *free* services to others—or at the very most, charge just a small amount for their services.

We are each on Earth to give back. Moreover, some of our deepest levels of fulfillment come from our giving to others. Yet, believing that it's morally or ethically *wrong* to use your strengths to become wealthy is like having a wound in one's belief system that needs healing.

This is the "*money-purpose wound.*" It results from thinking or believing that it is wrong to charge money whenever your actions express your purpose.

People with this wound often feel guilty when they charge to help others. Even making a small amount of money creates internal conflict within them. Because of their guilt, they often price products and services at the very low end of what they could charge.

This restricts their revenues and profits which wreaks havoc on their finances and often leaves them struggling to pay their bills. They have so many negative beliefs about becoming wealthy, it isn't even possible for them. Do any of these patterns sound familiar to you?

People who hold these limiting beliefs do not *yet* realize the inherent power and value of their true north. They have not yet accepted that their true north actually provides the clue to their ideal business and position within it.

To become abundantly wealthy, you *must* shift your thinking. You need to accept that you were born with the right to become prosperous. You deserve to be paid well for utilizing your talents to help customers.

You were not just born with the right to be wealthy, you were born with an internal guidance system—your passion, purpose, and strengths—the path which will lead to your riches.

This path is the business or vocation you were born to pursue. Not only does your true north reveal which type of business or profession you should pursue, it tells you which activities you are most qualified to perform as well as the ones you will most enjoy.

> You deserve to be paid well for utilizing your talents to help customers.

When pursuing your true north, realize the real issue isn't whether it is moral or ethical to utilize your purpose and strengths to be paid. The real issue is the *agreement* you made with the person you help.

If you agreed to help someone who came to you as a customer, then you each agreed to an exchange of value. You agreed to help them by using your skills and they agreed to pay you. This is the fundamental nature of all business transactions.

In the next two sections, you will identify your money beliefs and learn a method for rapidly shifting limiting money beliefs into empowering beliefs.

IDENTIFY YOUR MONEY BELIEFS

If you desire to grow a highly-successful business, attract more customers, or make profitable investments, then you must develop empowering money beliefs.

Your money beliefs are your personal views about money. You developed many of them as you grew up by accepting as true what you heard, saw, and experienced. This includes what your parents and family said and did, what you heard from your teachers, church, and role models, as well as what you observed of other people in your life and society.

You continue to develop money beliefs based upon the information you absorb through advertisements, your friends' or partners' comments, as well as through what you read and hear during your day. You will also develop beliefs about money based upon how you interpret your own experiences. This includes your internal dialogue about what occurs in your business and finances.

Your negative money beliefs hold
you back from achieving millionaire wealth!

Most of your money beliefs are outside of your awareness. Until you take time to consciously review them, you don't even know what your money beliefs are or how they run the financial part of your life.

Your money beliefs cover several areas, such as: are you worthy and deserving to have a lot of money; is it wrong or evil to make money; do you have the skills and ability to become a millionaire; are you smart enough to become rich; do you have enough education to make large amounts of money; do you think your past is hindering you from becoming wealthy; do you have the ability to keep the money you make instead of losing it; and will making money turn you into a greedy, bad, or selfish person?

> **Coaching:** Open your *Conscious Millionaire Journal*. Write down your money beliefs in each of the above areas. Put a checkmark by any beliefs that hold you back from attaining financial success. These are your *limiting money* beliefs.

Rapid Belief Change Technique

Quickly transform your limiting beliefs into empowering beliefs with this technique. I developed it based on more than two decades of study in the area of Neuro-Linguistic Programming (NLP). To use this technique, identify any limiting belief you want to change. Then transform it into an empowering belief by using this simple, yet powerful, seven-step technique.

Eliminate Limiting Belief

1. Acknowledge and write down what you are *gaining* by having this belief.

2. Acknowledge and write down what continuing to hold this belief is *costing* you.

3. Acknowledge and write down *counter-examples*: of people you personally know or who are public figures whose lives or businesses prove this belief is *false*.

CREATE EMPOWERING BELIEF

4. Write down a new, *empowering belief* that is opposite of your limiting belief.

5. Acknowledge and write down *examples*: when you either observed this new belief to be true or situations, that if they occurred, would prove it is *true*.

6. Acknowledge and write down all that you will *gain* by developing this belief.

TAKE POWERFUL ACTIONS

7. Choose a *specific goal* that the new empowering belief will help you achieve. *If you absolutely knew that you were going to achieve this goal*, what would be the first, second, and third actions you would take in the next twenty-four hours? Write them down and then take them. Then during the next thirty days, take at least three *conscious focused actions* each day to reinforce and fully install your new belief.

> **Coaching:** Open your *Conscious Millionaire Journal*. Utilize the Rapid Belief Change Technique™ to transform each limiting money belief you identified in the prior section into an empowering money belief.

MINDSET OF HIGHLY-SUCCESSFUL ENTREPRENEURS

Based upon three decades of building and selling companies, coaching business owners, and observing top entrepreneurs, I've discovered that highly-successful entrepreneurs think with a different level of conscious awareness and insight. Three of the ways in which they think differently are: *provide massive value, deliver an amazing customer experience*, and *lead and delegate*.

Because they think in these ways, they naturally grow their businesses, make a bigger difference, and have more wealth to give back to society.

1. Provide Massive Value: Let's consider three possible ways of thinking about the value exchange between the seller and the buyer. Only one of these will result in maximum profits over the long term.

The first type of entrepreneur seeks to create a "fair exchange," such that for every one dollar of value they provide to their customer, the customer pays them one dollar in exchange. Initially, this sounds good and right, but as you will soon realize, it will not result in your highest profits.

The second type of entrepreneur thinks about value in terms of obtaining the "benefit of the bargain," an exchange in which they receive more value than they provide the customer. They often utilize deceptive, misleading marketing to manipulate the buyer into paying more than the actual underlying value of what they are purchasing.

Entrepreneurs who think this way may achieve rapid growth for awhile. But over time, this way of thinking does not result in sustainable profits. Word of mouth from an unhappy customer travels fast and often results in the entrepreneur's failure.

The third type of entrepreneur, those who are the most successful and make the most money over time, think about the value proposition completely differently. They seek to provide significantly greater value to their customer than they charge in return. They literally seek to provide five, ten, twenty, even 100 times or more in value than what their customer pays for the products or services.

> *Provide 10 to 100 times*
> *more value than the price you charge!*

This probably creates two questions in your mind right now: "Why" would they do this; and "how" do they accomplish this without going broke?

The *why* is simple: they want massive sales. And, they know that a happy customer who believes they received a great value will come back to buy more. They will also market for the business by telling others—who will also become a customer. The *how* is equally simple, although it may take some imagination or the development of specialized knowledge.

A high value product is one that has significantly greater value to the purchaser than the amount they paid to purchase it. *For example*: Imagine a simple garden weeding tool that both saves the customer time and helps them accomplish a task at a low cost versus other methods available. The tool might cost a dollar to produce, sell for twenty dollars, yet be worth ten times the price to the buyer in the *value* they receive.

Another method to produce high-value products is to use your expert knowledge, which is your high-value formula, process, or proven method. Is it unknown to the purchaser, and is therefore highly valuable to them. *For example*: Imagine a program that reveals a sales method for quickly doubling sales closings. The course might cost fifty dollars to reproduce, sell for two thousand dollars, yet be worth $100,000 in new sales in the first year. This provides a fifty-to-one value to the purchaser, in the first year alone.

Highly-successful entrepreneurs always seek to provide massive value to their customers. This is a major reason their customers both refer others and return to buy more—month after month, year after year.

2. Amazing Customer Experience: Highly-successful entrepreneurs understand that the customer's experience determines whether they are happy, continue to buy, and refer others—or become unhappy, stop buying, and bad-mouth the business.

Top entrepreneurs are obsessed with creating an experience for their customer that goes beyond simply delivering great service. Their focus is providing an exceptional mental, emotional, physical experience for their customer. Their goal is not only to provide an experience that fulfills the strongest desires of their ideal customer, but to far exceed *anything* that customer could experience from their competitors.

> At every touch point, provide an experience that makes each customer ecstatic to do business with YOU.

Like highly-successful entrepreneurs, become passionate about understanding your customer's inner reality, perceptions, values, mindset, and specific sensory ways in which they process their world. At every touch point, provide an experience that makes each customer ecstatic to do business with YOU.

Top entrepreneurs establish a singular goal when it comes to their customer. They make certain that each customer has an experience that not only meets their expectations, but exceeds them. To assure this occurs, they build a team and culture that is *customer-focused*.

They regularly survey customers to determine if their experiences surpass their expectations, and make them ecstatic. If not, the business needs to change the service and experience provided to customers. After making the changes, their service team must follow up to assure the customer is thrilled with their experience.

3. Lead and Delegate: Highly-successful entrepreneurs lead their business by establishing the visionary purpose and goals for their business, then delegate most of the duties related to actual execution. In the words of my mentor and friend, Gary Ryan Blair, entrepreneurs lead by focusing on "what" the business should be doing and "why" this is important, then delegate everything related to "how," which are the actions. In short, entrepreneurs choose the direction and make high level strategic decisions. Then they hire people with specific skills and "know how" to achieve the business goals by turning their vision into results.

A complimentary way to view the responsibilities as an entrepreneur comes from another friend and mentor, Quincy Ellis. Think of there being three distinct roles within any business:

- the *entrepreneur* determines the direction by choosing the "what/why";

- the *manager* organizes the "what/why" and "oversees how"; and,

- the *technicians* (employees and outsourced) are the action-takers; they are "how" the results get accomplished.

Now, there are two types of skills you may *not* choose to delegate.

- The first type is your *strengths* that you enjoy using and for which you receive *high-dollar pay*. These skills may include: setting the vision, developing strategies, noticing opportunities, marketing, closing major sales, and negotiation.

- The second type is what you are *passionate* about and most enjoy doing. These relate to the

> You are responsible for choosing the business direction and strategies. Hire an "execution team" to put these into action!

original reason you started the business; that is, you wanted do these activities. *Examples include*: coaching, cooking, gardening, photography, technology, sports, and licensed skills such as being a massage therapist or chiropractor.

Yet, before you decide to personally provide "hourly paid" services, consider that these may actually be "technician" level jobs, even though they are highly paid. Unless you truly love performing these activities, you may grow your business faster, and create higher profits, by delegating these. Then, only assume your entrepreneurial role.

Entrepreneurs who excel at delegating typically choose a narrow focus for their position. Then they let go of—and delegate—all *direct* responsibility for everything else. That is one of their secrets to achieving rapid growth and high levels of wealth. As the entrepreneur, you are responsible for choosing the business direction and strategies. Hire an "execution team" to put these into action.

How much you can invest in an execution team will depend on the stage of your business. However, even at a start-up stage, delegating some of the execution, even to a part-time virtual assistant, will free you to focus on making decisions and acting as the entrepreneur.

> **Coaching:** Open your *Conscious Millionaire Journal.* Select one of the above strategies. Then choose three *conscious focused actions* you could take during the next twenty-four hours. Begin implementing them in your business.

Conscious Focused Action Model

This is the eighth version of the foundational model, which is found in Chapter 2, *Formula for Creating Wealth.*

The conscious and focus levels interrelate by utilizing each of the words on the conscious level with each phrase on the focus level. *For example*: Utilizing "provide massive value" at the focus level, ask:

CONSCIOUS FOCUSED ACTION MODEL - 8

- "What result will *providing massive value* help achieve?" and, "Why is *providing massive value* to accomplish this result a priority?"

- "Who will benefit from *providing massive value* to achieve this result?" and, "Who will help *provide massive value* to attain this result?"

- "How can I best p*rovide massive value* to reach this result?"

Approach the other three levels—action, result, and learning—the same as in the foundational model. If you don't fully achieve your desired result, want to improve your process, or care to achieve your result at a higher level, then iterate. Review each level to determine what needs to change. Return to the conscious level and make the changes as you go through the model again. Then *test* the changes to determine if they are actually better.

CONSCIOUS MILLIONAIRE COACHING

Build Your Strategy

Open your *Conscious Millionaire Journal*. Write a three-step business strategy using *conscious focused action*. Develop your strategy utilizing the concept provided in the *conscious* step below. It is an important concept from this chapter.

1. Conscious: Develop a goal of increasing your sales by collaborating with another business. *For example*: "Select one business each quarter, and then collaborate with them to discover additional ways you can each increase sales."

2. Focused: As you focus on your goal, choose three actions that will help you begin to achieve it. Determine the precise order for your actions.

3. Action: During the next twenty-four hours, execute by taking your three actions.

Grow Your Business

In your *Conscious Millionaire Journal* make notes on how you utilize each of the following to grow your business:

• Identify one of your business practices that reflects a belief in scarcity. Replace the old practice with a new practice that reflects a belief in abundance.

• Choose a goal for your business, then identify any limiting beliefs that might prevent you from achieving it. Change them into empowering beliefs.

• Ask your team to identify their limiting money beliefs. Use the *rapid belief change technique* to help them turn them into empowering beliefs.

Create your journey

Here are three choices for what to read next. The first is to read another *conscious* section. The second is to read another *millionaire* section. The third choice is to *journey* through the book linearly, reading it chapter by chapter.

Conscious: You may want to review "The Formula for Creating Wealth" section in Chapter 2, *Formula for Creating Wealth*, before continuing to the next chapter.

Millionaire: Take a look at "The Power of Money" section in Chapter 11, *Achieve Financial Freedom*, before going to the next chapter.

Journey: Continue forward to Chapter 9, *Become a Conscious Leader*.

QR Codes / Links

Go to the membership site to view a coaching video that demonstrates how to use the *Rapid Belief Change Technique*. As an added bonus, download a form that lists the seven steps of the technique. Access the site now at: **ConsciousMillionaire.com/member**

BECOME
a CONSCIOUS
LEADER

*Leaders inspire others and
guide them to achieve amazing results!*

In this chapter, you learn a new model of leadership; one built on the Conscious Millionaire *Triple Win* approach: you, others, and society winning together. You will discover the three skills of a conscious leader, the importance of developing a visionary business purpose, and why conducting business with integrity contributes to business growth. You will also learn how to create high value for each stakeholder and the importance of building a result-focused business. In addition, you will discover the four keys to achieving super health and vitality as a leader. Lastly, you will utilize the *Conscious Focused Action Model* to move forward on your Conscious Millionaire Journey.

Conscious Millionaire Leadership

We have entered a new stage of leadership and it is expressed in the triple-win concept discussed in *Conscious Millionaire*. You win at your highest levels by helping both others and society win as well. The new conscious leader is aware of the essential interconnectedness of all life.

Further, Conscious Millionaire Leadership is vision driven. It is built on the view that we have a personal obligation to serve a greater purpose, a higher good, in how we do business and conduct our lives. It is only through serving this higher business purpose that we will ultimately derive our highest profits.

> Ask yourself what purpose your business serves. Then dig deeper and ask: "What purpose does my life serve?"

There is a spiritual aspect to this type of leadership because it connects you with other people at a deeper core level. In doing so, it requires more of you than has ever been required from our leaders. It requires that you ask yourself what purpose your business serves. More importantly, it requires you to ask, "What purpose does my life serve?"

What message do you want to send as a leader about what you believe is right and ethical? What standard do you want to set for what it means to conduct good business? When you think of your legacy, in what ways will others' lives and the world become better because of how you conducted yourself, both as a leader and entrepreneur?

Conscious Millionaire Leaders
inspire others with their vision of a better life.

Your life as an entrepreneur is one of the greatest callings you could possibly have. As an entrepreneur you recognize the opportunity to help transform the lives of your customers. You also have the opportunity to demonstrate what true leadership means both by the purpose you choose for your business, and by how that purpose benefits others and helps our world to become better.

THE 3 SKILLS OF CONSCIOUS LEADERS

You are reading *Conscious Millionaire* because you are passionate about making a difference and rapidly growing your business. You value touching your customers in a way that literally transforms them. And like all great leaders, you seek to attract others and draw them in to join you in achieving your vision.

To become a conscious leader and achieve exceptional results, develop and hone these three skills:

> **1. Envision:** a strong purpose that is truly visionary in scope.
>
> **2. Engage:** others to become your team members, strategic partners, and customers.
>
> **3. Execute:** along with your team to fully achieve your desired vision.

Conscious leaders develop a big vision of what is possible. Then they turn their vision into a powerful purpose used to drive their business. Leaders understand it is their responsibility to dream the future so vividly and communicate it so precisely that others will want to become a part of their team. It is only by building a strong team that you can make your important difference.

The primary driver for sustainable success in any business is a vision to make an important difference, one that goes beyond just making money. As the leader of your business, this must become your top priority: creating a business purpose that will so fully transform your customers, that they will also become raving fans who tell others.

Conscious leaders are aware that a powerful vision accomplishes nothing without telling others. Communicate your vision and passion for it in conversations with people you meet. Put it on your website and disseminate it all over the Internet. Communicate it to perspective employees and outsourced agents. Notice whether they talk and act as if your vision inspires them and they want to become a part of it.

> As a leader, you are the first evangelist and promoter of your vision

Engage with others in a way that ignites a fire inside of them. When you enthusiastically share your vision and connect with them at a heart level, they will not only want to help you achieve the vision, they will also begin to embrace it as their own vision. Let them know how important their contributions are to your business and what they can specifically do to energize and promote the vision.

As a leader, you are the first evangelist and promoter of your vision. Share it in a way that connects with your prospects' problems and desires. Infuse them with a deep desire to buy your products and become a part of your community. Make them feel like they belong in a way that matters to them.

Conscious leaders understand the importance of becoming focused and executing on their visions. How many people do you know who have a big idea for how something could become better? They talk about it all the time—yet they never execute. They are not leaders. They are not entrepreneurs. They are simply people with ideas. And ideas without action achieve nothing.

That is why it is so critical to develop the skill of executing effectively. Wake up in the morning ready to execute the priorities that will advance your vision. Execute to motivate others to join with you and help bring your vision fully to life.

Conscious leaders become *conscious* of an inner vision, engage others to *focus* on it, and take *action* to turn their vision into reality. These are the three skills you have been developing throughout *Conscious Millionaire*. Mastering these skills will make the difference between experiencing failure and achieving success.

Develop Your Visionary Purpose

Your business purpose is your outlook on the future. It is your view of how your business will help customers and, by helping your customers, benefit society. It is what you imagine your business will accomplish. Your purpose is what you want to do that is meaningful, significant, and truly matters. It reveals how you want to make a valuable contribution to your clients and the world.

> *Conscious Millionaire Leaders*
> *develop a visionary business purpose.*

One of the most significant differences between *First Stage Capitalism*, which is only concerned about making profits, and *Second Stage Capitalism* which combines purpose with profit, is the business purpose. First stage businesses often seek to exploit others and have uninspired purposes such as dominate their industry. Second stage businesses, such as Conscious Millionaire businesses, have a purpose designed to inspire and make a difference in the world.

If reading this makes your visionary purpose sound lofty, that's because it is. Your purpose must not only inspire you as the owner, but everyone on your team. It is interconnected with your profit motive in that, by making an important difference for your customers, you make more sales which contribute to profits. Likewise, as your business profits grow, your capacity to help more customers also expands.

To develop your purpose, begin with the difference you want to accomplish, something that you personally feel passionate about. Then extend that desire to define the bigger reason you want to be in business—the difference you want to make for your customers. Think of this in terms of how, specifically, your customer will be better as a result of receiving your service or using your product. Answer this question, "How will they have changed?"

Your visionary purpose connects your business with ideals, such as increasing the quality of your customers' life, making the world a better place, and solving social problems. By combining your visionary purpose and core business values with a strong brand promise, you will create a powerful strategy for building and growing your business.

> **Coaching:** Open your *Conscious Millionaire Journal*. Write your business purpose. Then identify three *conscious focused actions* you will utilize to turn your purpose into results that help others and grows your bottom line.

The Integrity Imperative

What does it mean to lead with integrity? I define integrity as leading your business in a way that is "good for your *customers*, good for your *business*, and good for your *values*." Let's look at each of these.

First, you are in business to serve your customers. When you act with integrity, you are honest with your customers in every contact with them. Your marketing conveys what is beneficial about your products without deceiving or misleading your prospects. In all communications with your customers, you only make honest statements.

Now, I want to let you in on a secret. At either a conscious or unconscious level, your prospects and customers will know if you are lying, cheating, manipulating, and using them. Somewhere inside, they will have a sensation and emotional feeling they can't trust you, even if they are not fully conscious of why. Over time, this will harm your relationship and erode their trust.

> It is your role as a leader to infuse your values into everything that you do.

Integrity goes beyond honesty. It also includes doing what is good for the customer by taking your customer's best interest to heart. This means only selling your customer what will actually make their life, business, or organization better. It means genuinely caring about them.

Second, you are also in business to serve your company's growth and profits. Your goals, strategies, and actions must be directed toward expressing your purpose, expanding your business, and growing your bottom line. As the leader of your business, it is your responsibility to execute in ways that cause your business to expand and thrive.

Third, you are in business to serve the values you have established. Think of values in this way: if your purpose is the heart of your business, then your values are the life-force flowing through your business' veins. You give real meaning to your business by choosing values that state what is important to you.

As a leader, it is your role to infuse your values into everything that you do, from the products you develop and the customer service you provide, to how you select team members and treat them after they are hired.

Why is conducting business with integrity an imperative? The answer is found in the very meaning of the word. The definition of integrity is: necessary, essential, required, unavoidable obligation. It is imperative because nothing exists in isolation. Everything and everyone in your business is *interrelated*.

You grow your business by serving your customers, and yet it is by growing your business that you have the opportunity to serve more of them. Likewise, your values are what your customers can expect from your business.

By making integrity one of your core business values and building a culture of integrity, you build a solid foundation for sustained growth and profits. When integrity is at the core of how you think about your business, you demand more from yourself as a leader because you are committed to keeping your word.

When integrity becomes your business standard, it denotes a way of life at your business. Simply put, it defines how you conduct business.

Coaching: Open your *Conscious Millionaire Journal.* Describe three ways you can infuse integrity into your business. Choose one of these and during the next twenty-four hours take three *conscious focused actions* to begin implementing it.

The 4 Keys to Super Health

It takes energy to make conscious decisions and become a great leader. It takes energy to grow a successful business and become wealthy. The more vitality you have, the better leader you can become, greater difference you can achieve, and more money you can make. This is why it is critical that you pursue a life that promotes super health. You need to be at peak health if you want to lead and achieve at your highest potential.

Without vitality, you won't lead effectively, become successful, or even enjoy life. You certainly won't be able to enjoy your ideal lifestyle. When you are tired and worn out, you can't achieve much, period. Put your health first and many things in your life will fall into place.

If you want to make an important contribution to our world and achieve millionaire success, then you must generate abundant energy so you can "fire on all cylinders." To excel as an entrepreneur, *consciously choose* a healthy lifestyle, one that supports your business success. This is the only way you can perform at your peak and achieve your maximum results each day.

> To excel as an entrepreneur, *consciously choose* a healthy lifestyle, one that supports your business success.

Do you lack the energy, focus, and passion necessary to lead others and build your business? Do you feel you are living halfway instead of fully? When you are physically out of shape and have a poor diet, you are more likely to feel sluggish and become sick.

By contrast, when you are physically in a healthy state, you have the energy necessary to lead, grow your business, and make your contribution to our world.

While writing this book, I gained more than 100 pounds in just over a year. The weight gain was related to the death of my father, who I deeply loved and was also my best friend. This resulted in a health crisis of my own. As part of my healing and moving toward health, I realized part of the weight gain had resulted from how I had approached food most of my life.

I consciously chose to make a shift from looking at food as a form of *entertainment and emotional relief* to seeing food as a source of *healing and nourishment*. This change in mindset was an important aspect of my new approach to health. Food became my fuel instead of my friend.

As important as the physical dimension is to health, which includes your diet, there are other dimensions for you to also consider. The second dimension, which is *mental*, influences your health by the thoughts you feed your mind. These not only include the habitual statements that you make to yourself, but also the messages you receive from the environment in which you *choose* to live.

A third dimension of health comes from your *emotions*. When you are positive and passionately excited by your activities, you not only support your immune system and health state, your enthusiasm and motivation provide a jet blast of energy. Positive, loving thoughts and emotions of gratitude boost your immune system.

There is also a fourth dimension of health and vitality. It is *spiritual*. When you feel spiritually connected to something that is bigger than you, a sense of purpose, a vision you want to achieve with your business and life, you feel energized to move forward.

Why? You want to attain your vision because it truly matters. You want to achieve something significant with your life.

Expressing gratitude unequivocally relates to health, vitality, and wealth in all areas. When you project an outlook of gratitude, you become deeply aware of the blessings you have received. As a result, you not only feel more grateful, you also feel more connected to those you love.

Acknowledging how grateful you feel, not only for what you already enjoy in your life, but also for what will be coming into your life, has an immense benefit to your health.

When you are grateful, you feel energized and ready to achieve your visionary purpose. This is true whether you are communicating your gratitude to other people, expressing your gratitude to your view of a higher power, or acknowledging your gratitude to yourself.

If you want to achieve full health and vitality, then include each of the following in your lifestyle. As with all health matters, consult with your physician or health advisor before embarking on any diet changes or beginning exercise programs. Some of the information in this section may not be suitable for you and your health situation.

1. Healthy Eating and Hydration: For many people, a healthy diet may include whole foods such as freshly harvested vegetables and fruits together with whole grains, fish, and small amounts of animal protein. For me, I've discovered that the healthiest way to live is to either completely, or significantly, eliminate foods that cause long-term health problems. These may include: sugar, white flour, processed and chemically enhanced foods, soda drinks, as well as large amounts of animal fats, caffeine, and excessive alcohol. In addition, drink filtered water throughout the day. Green tea is also healthy.

2. Exercise: Engaging in regular exercise is critical to a healthy lifestyle. There are three important types of exercise. *Aerobics* help your cardiovascular and lymphatic systems as well as increase your endurance and stamina. *Strength training*, through the usage of weights, adds stability to your core, increases your strength, and speeds up your metabolism due to increasing muscle mass. S*tretching* warms your body up prior to physical exercise and cools it down afterwards, as well as enhances your body's overall flexibility.

> To lead at your peak level, consciously choose to attain all four areas of vitality: physical, mental, emotional, and spiritual.

3. Energy Practice: I suggest that you develop an energy practice that includes one or more of these:

qigong, tai chi, yoga, or deep breathing. Performing one or more types of energy movements will help you consciously relax while also vitalizing your body in ways that promote holistic health. This is because energy practices involve the body, mind, heart, and soul. They also bring many people into a deeper spiritual connection.

4. Adequate Sleep and Recovery: In order to revitalize and achieve your optimum health, allow time to get adequate sleep so you can fully recover. For the typical person, seven to eight hours of sleep each day is ideal. To enhance the quality of your sleep, refrain from caffeine and eating at least two to three hours prior to sleep. As entrepreneurs, we are often driven to work long hours for days and weeks without a real break.

To attain sustained excellence, take one or more days away from your work each week. Your body, mind, emotions, and spirit need "down time." Vacations in places which support your rejuvenation and well-being are ideal for this. Refer to "End of Your Day: Revitalize and Refocus" section in Chapter 6, *Maximize Your Results Daily*, for detailed information on preparing for restful sleep.

Body, mind, emotion, and spirit combine to fuel your health and keep you moving forward as a conscious leader. Together, they create your energy state. If your energy is low, then you find it difficult to make conscious decisions. You simply don't have the fuel to activate all regions of your mind and to remain aware. Also, when your energy fluctuates, you usually find it difficult to stay focused and take consistent actions.

To lead at your peak level, consciously choose to attain all *four* areas of vitality: physical, mental, emotional, and spiritual. As all of energy is interrelated, generating one type of vitality gives you more overall vitality—each dimension of health influences all of the others.

Developing and maintaining vital health and fitness is the *foundation* for all the success you will have, both as a leader and an entrepreneur. Make a *conscious choice* today to develop a healthy life.

Commit to eating a diet high in vegetables and protein, exercising several times a week, creating an energy practice, and allowing adequate time to sleep and recover. Take a holistic approach to your health and well-being.

> **Coaching:** Open your *Conscious Millionaire Journal*. Write three *conscious focused actions* you will take during the next twenty-four hours to become more healthy and fit. Why are each of these important you?

Appreciate Your Stakeholders

The greater the value you provide each of your stakeholders, the more powerful will be your entrepreneurial future. Moreover, your ability to deliver value will determine how well you attract people, as well as any investment capital and loans needed, to accelerate your business growth.

The stakeholders are organized into three groupings that are based on the three conscious perspectives—*you*, *others*, and *society*. The following section provides a high-level view of how each stakeholder brings value to your entrepreneurial business.

You as Stakeholder

1. Owner-Entrepreneur: These are the primary stockholders or partners who bring the vision, drive, strategic direction, and the entrepreneurial spirit to the business. Owner-entrepreneurs invest their time, money, and skills to start and grow the business. They assemble the team and often manage the business during the early stages. Because they assume the greatest risk, they have the greatest potential for a financial return.

2. Investors and Lenders: Investors own stock and may also have liens on business assets. They are co-owners of the business. Although not immediately obvious, lenders also belong in this category. This is especially true in the case of small businesses as lenders often make loans because they believe in the management and owners. In effect, they function as "quasi-owners" due to their vested interest.

Others as Stakeholder

3. Team Members: Your team members consist of employees, independent contractors, and out-sourced employee/skilled individuals. They are your *execution team* who help develop products, provide services, and manage departments of the organization. They possess the "how to" skills necessary to grow your business. Top-level team members may also collaborate with owner-entrepreneurs to develop the strategies. Team members execute the goals and strategies to achieve the business "dual focus": attain its higher purpose and create profitable growth.

4. Customers: They receive the core benefit of the products, services, and experiences that your business provides. The best customers have a strong alignment with your business purpose and values; and instead of being detached buyers, they feel engaged with your brand and how you express it. Through their purchases, your business receives the revenues that pay for all of your investments and costs, thereby allowing you to grow and produce sustainable profits.

5. Suppliers: Your suppliers provide the products and services necessary for you to build, operate, manage, and grow your business. These include: technology; office supplies; creative and digital services; pre-assembled products, as well as the parts and raw materials needed to build products; distribution; and done-for-you services, such as marketing, selling, and even service delivery. One of the best ways to grow your business is to focus on your strengths, then utilize suppliers to execute in other areas.

SOCIETY AS STAKEHOLDER

6. Society and Community: Both the community in which you do business, as well as our larger society, provide infrastructure, such as roads; support systems, such as fire protection and utilities; and the rule of law, such as police and an agreed upon legal system necessary for you to conduct your business. Society also makes it possible for the people you need on your team to live and prosper.

7. Environment: The environment provides resources needed to operate your business. These include: land, weather, materials, and any other elements used to fuel productivity and output. All areas of the environment are related to the long-term success of a firm. Without a healthy and functioning eco-system, none of the stakeholders, from owner to employees to customers, can exist, let alone thrive.

There is a mutually-beneficial relationship between your business and each of your stakeholders. Each stakeholder provides value to your business and your business provides value to each stakeholder. In addition, there are interdependencies between the stakeholders. *For example*: Owner-entrepreneurs provide employment for team members who serve customers who in turn provide revenue and a profit potential to the business/owner-entrepreneur who pays the team members.

> **Coaching:** Open your *Conscious Millionaire Journal*. Describe the value your business provides to each of the *seven* stakeholders. Also describe the value each stakeholder provides to your business. *For example*: Your business may provide value to the environment by minimizing its carbon footprint, while the environment may provide your business with the natural resources necessary to manufacture products.

How to Lead for Results

One of the major differences between successful business leaders and those who are unsuccessful is that *all* successful leaders focus on results. Instead of focusing on hopes, dreams, and good intentions, they focus on whether they, their people, and their business achieve *results that can be directly measured.*

In thinking about results, I realized the old maxim "all that matters is results" is not completely accurate. Yet something kept gnawing at me. I couldn't help thinking there were missing pieces to this statement, important things left out. What I discovered is important to you as a conscious leader.

I became aware of the missing elements and realized there are actually three elements to achieving results:

1. **What:** result are your *conscious focused actions* designed to achieve?

2. **Why:** is this outcome so important that achieving it should be a priority?

3. **How:** will you achieve it, including will your actions express your values?

As a leader, it is your responsibility to answer each of these questions: "*What* results will I achieve, *why* are they important priorities, and *how* will my business achieve them?" This goes to the heart of what it means to be conscious as a leader.

If you want to make an important difference, if you want to build a business that achieves a greater good, and if you want to live a life that truly matters—then *focus on results*.

Business isn't just about making money, it is also about how you treat others, whether you lie, or if you harm society, which includes our environment.

> *Conscious Millionaires focus on*
> *achieving a high return on investment.*

Another critical aspect of leading for results is developing a consistent focus on receiving a *return on your investment* (ROI) of your time, money, and resources. This return can be measured in many ways: lives changed, profits achieved, and value to society.

Unfortunately, many business owners forget this aspect of leading. If you want to be successful and stay in business, then evaluate your results in terms of their positive ROI.

However, it is not just your ROI in terms of money that matters; it is also your ROI in terms of how well you achieve your purpose. Do you benefit your customers? Will your business help more people this year than last year? Is society made better because of your business?

Return on investment must be measured not just in the traditional sense of financial return, but also in terms of how well you achieve your purpose. The *dual focus* of a conscious leader is to achieve a higher business purpose and create higher profits. That is the core tenet in *Conscious Millionaire*.

Further, if your goal is to build a long-term successful business, then why you choose to achieve a result today must include thinking about why this will help you achieve your long-term goals for your business. How will you deliver more fully on your purpose? How will your profits and cash flow support you in growing your business? These are the questions that each conscious leader must face and answer.

> **Coaching:** Open your *Conscious Millionaire Journal*. Define a result you plan to achieve *this week*. Describe the *what*, *why*, and *how* of your result. Consider how achieving this result will create a greater good. Then take *conscious focused actions* to achieve it.

Conscious Focused Action Model

This is the ninth version of the foundational model, which is found in Chapter 2, *Formula for Creating Wealth*.

The conscious level and focus level interrelate by utilizing each of the words on the conscious level with each stakeholder on the focus level. *For example*: Utilizing "society" (in this example, the *community* stakeholder in society) from the focus level, ask:

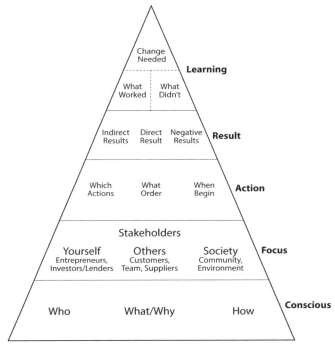

CONSCIOUS FOCUSED ACTION MODEL - 9

• "What result will be achieved by helping our *community*?" and, "Why is helping our *community* accomplish this result a priority?"

• "Who will help our *community* achieving this result?" and, "Who will help our *community* attain this result?"

• "How can I best help our *community* reach this result?"

Note: While it is clear that helping the community will benefit the overall community, what other stakeholders will also benefit?

Approach the other three levels—action, result, and learning—the same as in the foundational model. If you don't fully achieve your desired result, want to improve your process, or care to achieve your result at a higher level, then iterate. Review each level to determine what needs to change. Return to the conscious level and make the changes as you go through the model again. Then *test* the changes to determine if they are actually better.

CONSCIOUS MILLIONAIRE COACHING

Build Your Strategy

Open your *Conscious Millionaire Journal*. Write a three-step business strategy using *conscious focused action*. Develop your strategy utilizing the concept provided in the *conscious* step below. It is an important concept from this chapter.

1. Conscious: Consider the importance of *engaging* your team and customers. Develop a goal that supports you doing this regularly. *For example*: "Each week, engage both your team members and customers in a manner that makes them feel important."

2. Focused: As you focus on your goal, choose three actions that will help you begin to achieve it. Determine the precise order for your actions.

3. Action: During the next twenty-four hours, execute by taking your three actions.

Grow Your Business

In your *Conscious Millionaire Journal* make notes on how you utilize each of the following to grow your business:

• This week focus on execution, which is one of the three skills of great leaders. Select an important business goal for the week, then execute to achieve it each day.

• Develop one way to lead with integrity in your business (good for your customers, good for your business, good for your values). Then implement it.

• Choose three actions you can take to improve your diet or exercise this week, then take them.

Create Your Journey

Here are three choices for what to read next. The first is to read another *conscious* section. The second is to read another *millionaire* section. The third choice is to *journey* through the book linearly, reading it chapter by chapter.

 Conscious: You may want to review the "Conscious Millionaire Habit # 4—Do What's Right" section in Chapter 5, *Conscious Millionaire Habits*, before continuing to the next chapter.

 Millionaire: Consider reviewing the "Passion Ignites Your Fire" section in Chapter 4, P*assion, Purpose and Values*, before going to the next chapter.

 Journey: Continue forward to Chapter 10, *Build Powerful Relationships*.

QR Codes / Links

 Go to the membership site to view a coaching video that demonstrates how to develop your visionary business purpose. Access the site now at:

ConsciousMillionaire.com/member

BUILD POWERFUL RELATIONSHIPS

*With the right team, you can build
a high-profit business that changes the world.*

In this chapter, you learn how to consciously choose the people you want in your relationships and then network to find them. You will gain insight into the personal relationship needs of entrepreneurs and obtain techniques for leveraging your business relationships. Further, you will learn how to build your Conscious Millionaire team. You will also discover the seven keys to developing conscious relationships in business, ones that will be authentic and produce the highest results for all concerned. In addition, you will utilize the *Conscious Focused Action Model* to move forward on your Conscious Millionaire Journey.

CONSCIOUSLY CHOOSE YOUR RELATIONSHIPS

People who achieve at their peak make conscious decisions about their lives. They know what they want and how to achieve it. This includes consciously choosing with whom they associate, both personally and in business. They focus on building authentic relationships, ones that are right for each person in the relationship. In order to live and connect with others authentically, they choose to build relationships with people who are also committed to this level of relating.

This includes their business associates, trusted advisors, and investment professionals who help them with financial and retirement decisions. Consider how many people work hard only to lose their money because someone took advantage of them. Don't let this happen to you.

The first step in avoiding this type of experience is to consciously choose those to whom you trust with financial matters. This includes not only doing background checks, but also doing an internal check to determine if your intuitive sense is they are acting in your best interest—or only theirs.

The people you allow into your life will affect your wealth, success, and overall happiness. Further, your level of income and overall net worth will gravitate toward the average of the five people with whom you most closely associate.

*Consciously choose the
people in your business and life!*

What does this suggest? It implies that if you want to make a significant leap forward financially, then some of your closest relationships, including business coaches and mentors, should be significantly ahead of your current financial level. It also means you need relationships with other entrepreneurs who are at similar stages in their businesses and are also committed to becoming Conscious Millionaires.

This is true because each of you will be influenced by one another's values, priorities, goals, habits, and perhaps most of all, beliefs and mindsets. Together, you will create a group consciousness.

Whether that group consciousness helps or hinders your ability to achieve greater financial success will depend upon the people with whom you choose to associate. Positive people elevate you while negative people tend to depress you.

Furthermore, it isn't just the people with whom you do business that matter in your life. It's also important to consider carefully who you choose for friends, and the type of person you choose for romance or partnership. Their personal qualities and outlook on life will significantly influence you. They will either support or hinder you in achieving the success you desire.

Whether professional or personal, you will usually enjoy your best relationships with people who have similar values, goals, and standards.

You have two choices for how to build your relationships:

1. You could just *randomly* move through life with no real criteria for how you choose the people with whom you spend time; or

2. You consciously choose *criteria* for each type of relationship you want, then utilize the criteria to choose who to invite into your life.

The best way to develop criteria is to begin with the reason you want to build the relationship. What do you hope to gain through knowing a person? What do you want to accomplish together? In short, why do you want this person in your life? This could range from making money together to having fun to romance and companionship.

Similarly, seek to understand why they would want to associate with you and what they want from knowing you. What are the mutual benefits?

Given there are seven billion people on this earth, there is no lack of people who can fulfill any role or purpose in your life, whether financial or personal. Own your power by becoming conscious of why you want a specific person to share a part of your life.

It is a privilege that you ask anyone into your life, just as it is an honor they choose to be in your life. Likewise it is a privilege when someone asks you to be in their life; and it is an honor that you choose to be in their life. Consciously choose who you want in your life and why.

> It is a privilege that you ask anyone into your life, just as it is an honor they choose to be in your life.

In choosing your criteria, ask yourself if you genuinely enjoy and like the people you are associating with, *and* do they appear to enjoy and like you? Do you feel validated by them as a person and do you naturally validate them as well? Also consider whether you trust them, think they are honest, and share mutual respect.

If how you feel when you spend time with someone is important to you, then use it as part of your criteria for consciously choosing the people in your personal and financial life. *For example*: When you are together, do you feel depleted or more empowered? And, when you are apart, do you look forward to seeing them again or are you glad they are gone?

Successful people have a healthy level of what I call *self-interest*. This is your life. You have the right to choose with whom you associate. I also believe you have an obligation to respect others and seek mutual benefit from associating with them.

You may want to consider this list of criteria when selecting people with whom you associate personally, financially, or in business: enjoy one another, trust one another, share mutual validation and respect, interact well together, and demonstrate compatible values, priorities, standards, beliefs, and mindset.

Also consider if you complement each other by providing strengths the other is missing.

> **Coaching:** Open your *Conscious Millionaire Journal*. Write the names of your five closest relationships. What do you think is the average of their incomes and net worth? How close are those averages to what you seek? Is associating with them helping you move forward or holding you back?

Relationship Survival for Entrepreneurs

It is important that you discuss the demands of being an entrepreneur and owning a business with your partner or anyone you are dating. This is because the life of an entrepreneur is not a straight line to success. It is more like a roller coaster.

Therefore, the people with whom you enjoy your key personal relationships need to possess the personality to handle this type of ride. It is also important that they understand what they signed up for and are fully committed to your success as an entrepreneur. Even if they have their own career, by choosing to be in a relationship with you, they are on the entrepreneur journey with you.

If you have children, consider involving them in helping with the business as a way for them to participate and understand what it's like to be an entrepreneur and to learn from you.

> It is as if you have two marriages—one with your partner and another with your business.

I believe you will take the information in *Conscious Millionaire* and apply it to become highly successful. I know you will have amazing rewards as an entrepreneur. However, your journey requires patience and commitment. It is guaranteed to have ups and downs.

If you are like many entrepreneurs, it's like you have two relationships. It is as if you have two marriages—one with your partner and another with your business. This is why I am providing these guidelines to help you and your partner enjoy a thriving relationship while building and maintaining your successful business.

These guidelines are equally true without regard to gender, sexual orientation or ethnicity. If you are in a mutually caring and loving relationship with someone, the other person needs to feel important. So, to create a thriving relationship, nurture and pay attention to your partner on a regular basis. Below are guidelines:

1. Discuss with your partner, or anyone you are dating, the potential ups and downs of you being an entrepreneur and owning a business. Watch their response and listen to them in order to discover if this way of life "feels right" for them.

2. Openly communicate to your significant other any major business difficulties you may be experiencing, and if it seems right, discuss solutions together.

3. Regularly express your care, love, and concern to your partner or anyone you date, and ask the specific way *they* need you to express it (telling, touching, or showing through actions).

4. Provide time for them to communicate what they need to say, share their life and problems, and events of their day.

5. Share special times together; maybe a weekend away, dinner at a great restaurant, time alone at home—time just for the two of you.

Help your relationship thrive by showing your significant other that although your business is important, they are the most important person in your life. Not only is it imperative for your relationship, it is also critical to your financial success as an entrepreneur.

Experiencing conflicts with your partner because you failed to show them how important they are will drain your energy and sidetrack your focus. A thriving relationship with a partner can help you create a thriving business.

> **Coaching:** Open your *Conscious Millionaire Journal*. Write down what you want to discuss with your partner or significant other. If you are not in a romantic relationship, then plan to speak with a close friend. Establish a time for the two of you to discuss your priorities, commitments, and needs as an entrepreneur.

LEVERAGE YOUR BUSINESS RELATIONSHIPS

If you want to create massive wealth, then your most important resource is the people you know personally. Whether you are already financially successful and now seek even greater wealth, or are just beginning your millionaire journey, the people you know and your relationships with them, will make the biggest difference in how fast you achieve your financial goals.

You achieve your greatest results by building a support system and leveraging your relationships. To build this support, network. Schedule to attend business and social events, including seminars, trainings, and conferences, where there will likely be the type of people you prefer to meet.

Also join business, financial, and community groups that include members with whom you can network for mutual benefit.

Prepare for these events by making a clear list of *criteria* for *who* you want to meet and *why* you want to meet them. What are their characteristics? Show up at the events with a positive wealth mindset, then get in your *Millionaire Inner Zone* and become laser focused on your desired outcome.

Notice who you are attracted to and go right up to them. Engage them in a conversation. Focus on them, let them talk, and be a good listener. Always seek to understand what *they* want and how you can help them. As you listen, review your criteria for the relationship you seek and determine if they are a fit for you.

If they are, continue the conversation by sharing more about yourself. Remember that *authenticity* attracts people. Be yourself. Share what you value, what matters to you. Seek to find commonalities between the two of you.

Discuss your vision for what you want to accomplish: the difference you want to make, the products or services you are bringing to market, any new business directions you are exploring. Look for opportunities that could be of mutual benefit.

Conscious Millionaires
walk into the room laser focused!

Within twenty-four hours after the event, follow up with them by sending a note, email, or phone call. Make them feel important and tell them how much you enjoyed meeting them. This is how you begin or extend your circle of influence. It is also how you turn yourself into a *person of influence*. If you want to create high levels of wealth, becoming a person of influence should be one of your goals.

Who is a person of influence? You instinctively know the answer. They hold strong influential ties with many of the most important people in your industry or community.

As you expand both the quantity and quality of the people in your network, you can emerge as a person of influence. One of the fastest ways to do this is always focus on others and how you can help them.

As you build your circle of influence, the great news is that each person you know has their own circle of influence. This means you can leverage both circles.

For example: Make a list of the names of people you want to meet. Choose one of these names and ask the people you know if they, or anyone they know, are personally connected with that person. Keep asking until you find someone who has a connection with the person you want to meet.

Then ask them to make an introduction. Why? Your credibility will be much higher if you meet a person through a mutual acquaintance than if you seek them out yourself.

> **Coaching:** Open your *Conscious Millionaire Journal*. Write a list of specific criteria for the type of person you want to meet at your next networking meeting. Develop three questions you can utilize to determine within sixty seconds if someone fits your criteria. Use these at the event.

Your Conscious Millionaire Team

To build an effective team, first know yourself: your passion, values, vision, and strengths as well as your weaknesses. All of these need to be considered. Throughout *Conscious Millionaire*, you have been developing a more complete understanding of who you are and what you want to achieve.

> *Create specific criteria for*
> *whom you want on your team.*

The starting place for building your team is to decide what specifically you want your team to accomplish: start a new business, run a franchise, grow your current business, innovate to develop new products, buy and sell real estate; whatever you want to achieve as an entrepreneur.

Next, make a list of all the skills and talents you will need among your team members so you can achieve your entrepreneurial goals. Create a picture of your ideal team. Now compare what you bring to the table against the list. Notice what is still missing. These are the characteristics and skills of the people you will need in order to build your ideal millionaire team.

In a broad sense, everyone who in any way helps you to achieve your vision, build financial success, and create the life you desire is a team member. If someone believes in you and wants you to become successful, think of that person as a team member. This includes the person who cuts your hair, cleans your house, or is your personal fitness trainer. Be *grateful* they are part of your life and believe in you.

However, the people with whom you will interact on a regular basis, share decision-making power, and collaborate with on business or financial projects are your Conscious Millionaire Inner Circle. These people have a vested interest in your success because in an important way, their financial success is either directly or indirectly related to yours. Together, you are working toward a common goal—one of making a difference in the marketplace that results in high profits.

How? By helping a specific type of person, such as an entrepreneur, mom, student, professional, or business owner, solve a problem or achieve something they desire. This is how you and your team bring value to the world.

Consciously choose your inner circle based on how you can each benefit one another. Consider how they can contribute to your overall vision and results—and how you can contribute to their vision and results as well. How can you both win by associating together? How will your team help other people and society win as well?

Consciously choose your millionaire inner circle based on how you can each benefit one another.

In order to develop your optimum team, constantly provide opportunities for each of your team members to grow, evolve, and achieve whatever is important to them.

While all of your inner circle members share a common interest, they may not have a common background or similar personalities. A diversity of experience, perspectives, and risk tolerances often leads to a more robust collaboration and a wider range of insights.

Validating one another's thoughts, input, and value to the team is critical in creating a commitment and camaraderie among members. Your inner circle should be people who listen to and support you as well as one another. To build a strong team, both you and all members, must constantly focus on earning one another's trust.

Conscious Relationships in Business

Business relationships that are conscious emphasize the value, contribution, and responsibility of each person. It is about partnering for the common good of all those involved; it is a about turning mutual benefits into mutual results.

In your relationships with business partners, investors/lenders, customers, your team, suppliers, or anyone else with whom you do business, you each benefit from consciously expressing your expectations.

Imagine having business relationships in which you feel free to say what you think, rather than avoiding topics that may be emotionally uncomfortable. Because you and the people with whom you work are in a conscious relationship, it is important that you establish an agreement that you can honestly discuss whatever occurs. Straightforward communication is critical to business success.

You are clear with one another about what you want and expect. When you have conflict, openly discuss your perspectives on it and how you can reach new agreements that work for each of you.

> At any time, there is a right way, which you could also think of as a best way, for you to relate with each person in your life.

Imagine being in business relationships in which everyone is committed to a common vision. You openly share ideas and resources so you can more productively collaborate with one another. This is what can occur when you build conscious relationships.

There are seven keys to building conscious relationships in business:

1. Conscious Communications: To become conscious is to become *aware* of what is true in terms of what you and others want, what is actually being said in discussions, and the personal dynamics that are occurring. When you relate consciously, you have the courage to both share and listen to what is true for one another. *For example*: Have a conversation with someone on your team, during which you each openly express what is important to you.

2. Clear Expectations: To build a strong relationship, one that is founded in honesty, trust, respect, and authenticity, each person in a relationship must become conscious of what they want and expect, and then openly communicate it. *For example*: Tell your employees or team members what you want and expect; then give each of them time to tell you what they want and expect as well. Write these down so each person knows what to expect.

3. Right Relationships: At any time, there is a right way, which you could also think of as a best way, for you to relate with each person in your life. What feels right to you may change in the future as situations shift and evolve. Ways of relating may include one or more dynamics, such as friend, romance, or business. *For example*: In each of your relationships, notice which ways of relating feel right for you at this time. Ask the other person what ways feel right for them. Then make a conscious decision together about how you will relate.

4. Mutual Responsibilities: Relating consciously requires each person to uphold their part of the relationship. This includes responsibility for keeping their commitments and respecting others in the relationship. *For example*: Only make commitments you plan to honor, and unless something occurs beyond your control, make it your habit to always keep your word; and ask that others act under the same guidelines.

5. Personal Boundaries: Conscious relating can only occur when you respect other people's boundaries and they respect yours. Think of boundaries as the dividing line between who you are and who others are; your needs, desires, and feelings reside within your boundaries. *For example*: Become conscious of your boundaries, like topics you will discuss, then clearly communicate your boundaries and how you want them respected. Be aware of the boundaries others establish and respect them as well.

 6. Power Dynamics: There are five ways in which power can be distributed in any relationship: you lead, the other person leads, alternate power, divide power, or collaborate. There is no one ideal way to divide or share power. The right way is the one that works for all those involved at any time and in any circumstance. *For example*: Select one of your business relationships. Openly discuss power dynamics and choose the one that best supports achieving the agreed goals.

7. Resolving Conflicts: It is impossible for relationships to have no conflicts. This is true because conflicts are caused by differences in values, priorities, goals, or even perspectives on what occurs. Rather than resulting in a tragedy, conflicts can become opportunities for building closer bonds. *For example*: When a conflict occurs with someone, ask for a "time out" so neither of you push the other's emotional buttons nor escalate the conflict. Allow time for each of you to reflect. Then, openly discuss what occurred and how you can reach a solution.

Consider how you can apply these principles to your business relationships. In your connection with clients or customers, you have a vested interest in communicating clearly and working together to resolve any conflicts. Likewise, your customer has a vested interest in communicating their needs and working with you to resolve conflicts. It is in each of your best interests to create a productive relationship.

In your relationships with business partners, employees, suppliers, lenders, or anyone else with whom you do business, you each benefit from consciously expressing your expectations. You also benefit from keeping your commitments and resolving conflicts in a way that respects each of your best interests.

By creating business relationships consciously, you expand what is possible. You not only discover more ways to grow your business, you also develop richer and more productive business relationships.

> **Coaching:** Open your *Conscious Millionaire Journal*. Select one of the seven keys and describe how to utilize it to grow your business. During the next twenty-four hours, take three *conscious focused actions* to begin implementing it in your business.

CONSCIOUS FOCUSED ACTION MODEL

This is the tenth version of the foundational model, which is found in Chapter 2, *Formula for Creating Wealth*.

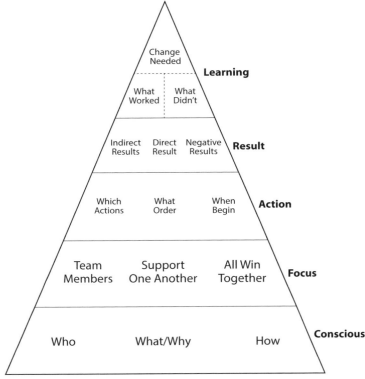

CONSCIOUS FOCUSED ACTION MODEL - 10

The conscious level and focus level interrelate by utilizing each of the words on the conscious level with each focal point on the focus level. *For example*: Utilizing "support one another" from the focus level, ask:

- "What result will *supporting one another* help achieve?" and, "Why is *supporting one another* to accomplish this result a priority?"

- "Who will benefit from the team *supporting one another* to achieve this result?" and, "Who on the team will *support one another* to attain this result?"

- "How can the team best *support one another* to reach this result?"

Approach the other three levels—action, result, and learning—the same as in the foundational model. If you don't fully achieve your desired result, want to improve your process, or care to achieve your result at a higher level, then iterate. Review each level to determine what needs to change. Return to the conscious level and make the changes as you go through the model again. Then *test* the changes to determine if they are actually better.

CONSCIOUS MILLIONAIRE COACHING

Build Your Strategy

Open your *Conscious Millionaire Journal*. Write a three-step business strategy using *conscious focused action*. Develop your strategy utilizing the concept provided in the *conscious* step below. It is an important concept from this chapter.

1. Conscious: Create a goal that supports team members acknowledging the contributions of one another. *For example*: "Hold weekly meetings, and during these allow time for members to express their gratitude to other team members for specific contributions." *Note*: Even if you have only one person helping you, schedule a time each week for the two of you to express gratitude to one other.

2. Focused: As you focus on your goal, choose three actions that will help you begin to achieve it. Determine the precise order for your actions.

3. Action: During the next twenty-four hours, execute by taking your three actions.

Grow Your Business

In your *Conscious Millionaire Journal* make notes on how you utilize each of the following to grow your business:

• Before you attend your next business event, develop specific criteria for who you want to meet. Then practice your networking skills by finding at least three people who meet your criteria.

• Consciously choose your team members by deciding what types of people you need; utilize your connections to find them.

• Teach one of the keys to conscious relationships to your team; then use it as a guide for how you relate with one another this week.

continued

Create Your Journey

Here are three choices for what to read next. The first is to read another *conscious* section. The second is to read another *millionaire* section. The third choice is to *journey* through the book linearly, reading it chapter by chapter.

 Conscious: You may want to review the "Identify Your Core Values" section in Chapter 4, *Passion, Purpose and Values*, before continuing to the next chapter.

 Millionaire: Consider reviewing the "Your Millionaire Standard" section in Chapter 6, *Maximize Your Results Daily*, before going to the next chapter.

 Journey: Continue forward to Chapter 11, *Achieve Financial Freedom*.

QR Codes / Links

 Go to the membership site to view a coaching video on how to build your Conscious Millionaire team. Access the site now at:

ConsciousMillionaire.com/member

ACHIEVE FINANCIAL FREEDOM

*You must possess money to
enjoy life at your highest levels!*

Making millions of dollars does *not* guarantee financial freedom. Worse, it doesn't even protect you from becoming bankrupt. In order to achieve financial freedom, not only do you need to understand how to make money, you must also learn how to *keep* it. This chapter will reveal the real power of money which includes living well, helping others, and making a powerful difference in our world. Further you will learn the habits and financial strategies necessary to become financially free. You will also discover how to use your risk factors to achieve superior financial returns. In addition, you will utilize the *Conscious Focused Action Model* to move forward on your Conscious Millionaire Journey.

The Power of Money

You picked up this book because you want to become wealthy. Indeed, the desire to be rich is a noble one, especially when coupled with the desire to make a difference. It takes money to pay your living expenses, buy a home or car, and purchase food, education, and entertainment.

If you want to surround yourself with beauty, travel to exotic places, or enjoy the finer things in life, you must have money. If you want to create free time to enjoy your life and be with the people you care about, you must have money. If you want to be free from financial worries, live well without working, or prepare for your retirement, you must have money to invest.

Money can be a
powerful force for good.

Money also empowers you to do amazing good for others and contribute to making this a better world. What differences will you make by how you use your money? Will you pay for your children's college or help an aging parent or relative? Do you desire to support non-profit organizations and causes you care about? Have you considered using your wealth to start your own foundation as a way to create your personal legacy?

Money is power!

It provides the power to build and grow your business, develop new products to help your clients, and invest for your future. Money provides the power to live as you choose, help those you care about, and give back to the world.

People who both become and remain financially free have the power to both live well and help others.

If your goal is to enjoy financial freedom, then study how to create wealth: read books, listen to audio programs, and attend financial success and business programs on a regular basis; then apply what you learn by taking *conscious focused action*.

Unfortunately, possessing a large annual income or even making millions from selling a business or doing well with your investments, won't guarantee financial freedom. You can build a highly-profitable business and still end up broke.

> *Money* provides the power to live as you choose, help those you care about, and give back to the world.

Why? The answer is probably immediately clear. Think of all the people who become rich and ultimately appear in the headlines for going bankrupt, even after making tens or hundreds of millions of dollars. Have you ever wondered how they managed to lose all of that money?

They never developed responsible money habits or sound financial strategies. As a result, they failed to multiply their wealth because they made bad business and investment decisions by paying little to no attention to risk. Use the information in this chapter to make certain this never happens to you.

This can include trusting the wrong people to take care of their money or advise them on their financial decisions. Instead of choosing to enjoy the luxury life they could actually afford, they squandered their money living at even higher levels.

Your life doesn't need to turn out that way. By using the money habits, financial strategies, and information you are about to learn, you can take the money that you make in your business and use it to create financial freedom. As a result, you can also enjoy the financial security you seek.

I'm providing you with the information in this chapter because making a lot of money, even millions or tens of millions, does *not* guarantee you'll become financially free. Worse, it doesn't guarantee you won't end up penniless.

The 3 Uses of Money

As you make money and grow your wealth, consider the three specific purposes for having money. Also, contemplate how much wealth you actually need and honestly want to enjoy your life. These are the three uses of money: *pay for your lifestyle*, *invest for your future*, and *give back to others*. This is a more complete explanation of each:

1. Pay for Your Lifestyle: You require money to pay for your lifestyle; this includes your homes, cars, vacations, food, and personal needs such as medical and clothing. It also includes education for you and your family—college, training courses, business and financial success books, audio programs, videos, seminars, mentoring, and coaching.

The amount of money you have determines whether you take your vacations at two-star economy hotels and frequent low cost places to eat *or* enjoy the amenities of five-star luxury resorts and dine at fine restaurants. It also determines whether you constantly struggle to pay your bills and provide for your family *or* can easily afford your desired lifestyle and are free from financial stress, that wears you down.

2. Invest for Your Future: You will need money if you want to start or expand your business, or engage in any type of entrepreneurial activity. You will also require financial capital in order to invest for each stage of your life. Estimate now how much you will need for each additional decade you expect to live. Saving and investing regularly must be a part of your financial life if you are going to prepare for a quality future—one in which you are financially secure.

You can invest for specific future events, like major family vacations, children's education, or your non-working retirement years. It is also possible to invest and grow your financial wealth to the level that you are financially free so you never need to work again. The money produced from investments can also help pay for your lifestyle and be used to give back to others.

> The goal of your life is to enjoy a whole life, not spend your whole life making money.

3. Give Back to Others: Consider the differences you can make by accruing more financial resources to support causes that matter to you. By creating financial wealth, you increase your power to provide for others and make a significant change in the world. You can not only contribute *money* to causes you care about, and as you become financially free, you will also have more *time* to contribute.

Have you ever wondered what it would be like to have the ability to write a check any time you want to help someone in need or give to a charity? Imagine the massive difference writing a big check such as $10,000, $100,000, or even $1,000,000 could make. Now imagine yourself writing it and notice how you feel as your pen writes those numbers on the check and then you sign it. Thinking of money in this way, you become conscious of its positive power when used for the good and betterment of humankind.

Once you are aware of the three uses of money, then you only have two questions to answer. First, how much money do you want annually for each of these uses? Second, do you want to continue to work in order to provide this money (active income) or do you want to own investments that provide you with this money (passive income)? Consider these questions as you read this chapter.

What is your personal
definition of financial freedom?

For some people, financial freedom means possessing enough money so that they never need to work again, except for whatever work is necessary to oversee their investments. For others, financial freedom is more psychological in nature. It means never worrying or stressing about money. They may work simply because they enjoy their activities. However, they have savings and investments so they feel financially secure even without their work income.

A few years ago, my friend, Mary Goldenstein and I had a conversation about abundance and how much money any person actually needs to live as they choose. We remarked that we live in a world in which we are taught to always want more. As a result, many people develop a belief that they never have enough, no matter how much financial wealth or level of success they achieve.

The more we discussed this phenomenon, the clearer it became that one reason many people never develop precise financial goals is they can't settle on an actual dollar amount that would be sufficient—enough. Out of this realization came a phrase that we coined together: "sufficient abundance." This doesn't mean you should "limit" your wealth or that having abundant prosperity is wrong in any way.

What it does mean is there is an amount of financial wealth that is sufficient to support your desired lifestyle, level of investing, and desire to give back.

Think of *sufficient abundance* in this manner: the goal of your life is to enjoy a whole life, not spend your whole life making money.

> **Coaching:** Open your *Conscious Millionaire Journal*. Determine how much money you will need for each of the three uses of money. Then decide whether you want to continue working (active income), develop investment income (passive income), or combine active and passive approaches to create this money/cash flow.

Conscious Money Habits

One of the biggest differences between entrepreneurs who achieve financial freedom and those who don't is their money habits. There are responsible and irresponsible money habits. Conscious Millionaires develop responsible money habits; ones that help them become rich and enjoy living fully.

By contrast, entrepreneurs who are financially irresponsible, constantly struggle to make money. As a result, they often experience emotional stress.

*Conscious Millionaires
take responsibility for their finances!*

These are seven proven money habits. You may not be able to establish all of them at once, but you can develop them over the next six to twelve months. Your habits define your path in life. Take the path to financial freedom by developing these money habits.

These are the seven conscious money habits for achieving financial freedom:

1. Spend less than you make: Total expenses, including credit payments, should be less than your after-tax income. This is your first step.

2. Live on a budget: To create a strong financial future, have a budget and consistently use it to track your revenues and expenditures.

3. Save at least 10 percent: From each paycheck (or company withdrawal) deposit at least 10 percent of your after-tax income into long-term savings and investments. If you can't start with 10 percent, establish a set percentage amount and increase it as you can.

4. Maintain an emergency fund: In addition to your other savings and investments, create a cash fund that should cover six to twelve months of usual expense.

5. Give back regularly: Giving money to others sends a message to your mind that you have plenty of money to both pay for your life and help others.

6. Pay cash for most depreciable assets: Don't use credit cards, lines of credit, or home equity loans to buy things that go down in value, except for big ticket items such as cars, motor homes, and boats. Pay cash for other items that depreciate, such as home and personal electronics, household goods, sports equipment, or clothes.

7. Pay off your credit cards each statement: Do you run up credit card bills you can't pay off? Don't pay for vacations, gifts, or entertainment with a credit card unless you are capable of fully paying for those charges when the credit payment is due. If you can't afford to pay for it in thirty days, don't purchase it.

ACHIEVE FINANCIAL FREEDOM 219

Coaching: Open your *Conscious Millionaire Journal*. For each of the seven habits, write one *conscious focused action* you will take during the next three days to begin developing it. Which habits do you most want to develop?

Conscious Millionaire Financial Strategies

If you want to create a life of financial freedom and be able to enjoy all the amazing lifestyle possibilities available to you, then understand and apply sound financial strategies to your business, financial, and personal life. Based on three decades of learning what works and what doesn't, I developed seven financial strategies. I personally use these strategies and teach them to my clients.

> Understand and apply sound financial strategies to your business, financial, and personal life.

If you want to move into the fast lane of financial freedom, I suggest you begin by choosing three of these principles—whichever three grab your attention. Focus on mastering these and you will increase the speed with which you achieve financial freedom:

1. Create massive wealth by providing massive value: Create and/or deliver products and services that eliminate one of your customer's painful problems or help them attain their strongest desires; provide substantially more value than you charge.

2. Choose opportunities that match your values, goals, and business purpose: There are infinite opportunities. Choose the ones that reflect your values and business purpose. These are the ones right for you. Leave the others for someone else.

3. Take actions that go with the flow, not against it: Being in sync with the natural direction of life and trends, increases the speed and ease with which you build wealth.

4. Consider both the downside risk and upside potential: When an investment has the potential to make higher than average returns, it also has the risk of experiencing larger than average losses. Always consider both.

5. Make financial decisions that fit your risk comfort range: If the risk is beyond your emotional tolerance, you will tend to reverse your decision if you have losses or cut your profits short by selling too early.

6. Always consider timing before making a financial decision: There is a natural timing to opportunities. If you are too early, the world may not yet be ready for your idea; if you are too late, you miss the trend and the big opportunity!

7. Check your instincts before acting: If something doesn't feel right, it may simply be the wrong direction for you. However, it could also be that just one or two elements need to change. *For example*: The timing, people involved, or location may need to shift, and if they do, this may turn into a financial opportunity.

> **Coaching:** Open your *Conscious Millionaire Journal*. Select one of the financial strategies. Write three *conscious focused actions* you could take in order to implement this strategy in your business. Take these actions during the next twenty-four hours.

Know Your Risk Factors

Entrepreneurs who achieve financial success, and then keep their money once they make it, understand risk. Conscious Millionaires determine the risk factors *before* making investments. As circumstances change, they also re-evaluate the risks to determine if they need to alter their financial decisions.

risk = probability of not achieving desired result

The problem is most people only evaluate risk by focusing on all the positives they hope will occur. Worse, they pay little or no attention to determining the likelihood, or probability, that instead of reaching their profit goal, they actually incur losses. This often results from not understanding the full risk.

Most people think about risk incorrectly; they view it as indicating what might go wrong. A better way to define risk is as the probability you will *not* achieve the financial result you desire.

During a long time period, what investment analysts call a time horizon—for instance fifty years—the overall United States stock markets have returned just over 10 percent on an annualized basis.

Therefore, if a typical stock only returns 10 percent in an average year, for a stock to earn 30 percent per year for several years in a row, would be rare. Why? Because this is three times the average long-term annualized yield. Therefore, there is a high risk that the stock will not achieve this level of return.

Unfortunately, most people only focus on the excitement of the hoped for 30 percent profit for ten years without every considering there is a *high risk*, or probability, this would not occur.

If you make your financial decisions without considering the real risks, there is a *high risk* you won't become a millionaire.

Or if you do, you'll eventually lose your money and never have the financial freedom you desire! To achieve financial freedom, pay close attention to risk.

I developed three risk factors to help you evaluate risk. It is important that you consider each of these *before* making any major business decision or financial investment. Then reconsider them at regular intervals for as long as you own your business or investment.

In each of these risk factors, a rating of "one" is conservative and a rating of "ten" is highly risky. Therefore, the more you choose options that are toward the one rating, the less likely you will be exposed to risk. Below are the three risk factors:

1. Your Risk Appetite: This is your natural comfort level with taking financial risk. Honestly rate yourself from one to ten. A rating of "one" means you are very conservative: that is, you are uncomfortable losing any money. A rating of "ten" means you are willing to lose all of your investment. The higher your risk appetite, the more you are emotionally comfortable with assuming risk. Most entrepreneurs, but not all, have risk appetites of six or higher. This is because being an entrepreneur is a highly risky endeavor.

2. The Event Risk: Every financial decision or investment has an inherent level of risk, which is the probability your desired result will not occur. Rate each financial decision with a one to ten; "one" meaning it is almost certain the desired result will occur, and "ten" meaning it is almost certain that it won't occur. *For example*: If you place $1,000 into an FDIC insured, federally insured, one-year CD at 5 percent

> Considering choosing people with different risk appetites and investment styles on your business or investment team.

annual interest ($50 interest income in a year), you have an event risk factor of one because there is a high probability of realizing $1,050 in a year—your original $1,000 plus $50 of interest income. If you have a low risk tolerance, you will tend to choose investments with a low event risk.

Conversely, if you have a high risk tolerance, you will gravitate toward investments with a higher event risk. What level of risk are you willing to take?

3. Your Risk Management: This is your active management of risk. Rate your management from one to ten. A low score of "one" means you actively pay attention to your investments, regularly review the risks, and actively manage them by making new decisions whenever needed. A high score of "ten" indicates you pay no attention to your investments, ignore details, and fail to properly manage your investments. You also fail to make risk decisions when circumstances change.

Consider choosing people with different risk appetites and investment styles on your business or investment team. They often balance one another and reach better overall decisions. However, be certain that the person who is ultimately responsible for an investment decision has an active management style so they pay attention to changing circumstances and make new risk-related decisions whenever needed.

Conscious Focused Action Model

This is the eleventh version of the foundational model, which is found in Chapter 2, *Formula for Creating Wealth*.

CONSCIOUS FOCUSED ACTION MODEL - 11

The top tier and bottom tier of the conscious level interrelate by utilizing each of the *uses of money* on the top tier with each of the words on the bottom tier. *For example*: Utilizing "investing" from the top tier, ask:

- "What result will *investing* help achieve?" and, "Why is *investing* to accomplish this result a priority?"

- "Who will benefit from my *investing* to achieve this result?" and, "Who will help me invest to attain this result?"

- "How can I best *invest* to reach this result?"

Note: Having your desired *lifestyle* will clearly benefit you. Who else will it benefit?

The focus level changes by including three factors that help you achieve financial goals: *conscious money habits*, Conscious Millionaire *financial strategies*, and the *risk factors*.

Approach the other three levels—action, result, and learning—the same as in the foundational model. If you don't fully achieve your desired result, want to improve your process, or care to achieve your result at a higher level, then iterate. Review each level to determine what needs to change. Return to the conscious level and make the changes as you go through the model again. Then *test* the changes to determine if they are actually better.

CONSCIOUS MILLIONAIRE COACHING

Build Your Strategy

Open your *Conscious Millionaire Journal*. Write a three-step business strategy using *conscious focused action*. Develop your strategy utilizing the concept provided in the *conscious* step below. It is an important concept from this chapter.

1. Conscious: Consider the importance of developing a budget for your business. Create a goal of eliminating unnecessary expenditures. *For example*: "Develop a budget and review it weekly and monthly."

2. Focused: As you focus on your goal, choose three actions that will help you begin to achieve it. Determine the precise order for your actions.

3. Action: During the next twenty-four hours, execute by taking your three actions.

Grow Your Business

In your *Conscious Millionaire Journal* make notes on how you utilize each of the following to grow your business:

continued

- Choose one of the "Conscious Millionaire Financial Strategies" and use it in your business this week.

- Determine the annual income you need in order to provide for all three uses of money combined. Utilize this information when establishing financial goals for your business.

- Rate your personal risk appetite from "one" to "ten." Then utilize this knowledge to consciously choose the type of business investments you make.

Create Your Journey

Here are three choices for what to read next. The first is to read another *conscious* section. The second is to read another *millionaire* section. The third choice is to *journey* through the book linearly, reading it chapter by chapter.

Conscious: You may want to review the "Wealth with Speed and Ease" section in Chapter 7, *Your Millionaire Inner Zone*, before continuing to the next chapter.

Millionaire: Consider reviewing the "Identify Your Money Beliefs" and "Rapid Belief Change Technique" sections in Chapter 8, *Create an Abundance Mindset*, before going to the next chapter.

Journey: Continue forward to Chapter 12, *Develop Your Business Model*.

QR Codes / Links

Go to the membership site and view a coaching video about how to avoid risk pitfalls. As an added bonus, download a list of the three risk factors. Access the site now at: **ConsciousMillionaire.com/member**

DEVELOP YOUR
BUSINESS MODEL

*To achieve your higher purpose,
you must develop a robust business model.*

In this chapter, you discover the three compelling reasons for owning a business: your lifestyle, purpose, and exit plan. In addition, you will learn the inside-out approach to designing your business and how to make a transformational difference for your customer. You will discover the nine keys to conscious profits and how to utilize the *Conscious Millionaire Business Model™* to design your ideal business. This model helps existing and start-up businesses make a bigger difference and create bigger profits. You will also utilize the *Conscious Focused Action Model* to move forward on your Conscious Millionaire Journey.

THE NEW WAY TO MAKE MONEY

The traditional approach to building a business only focuses on *how* to make money, without any real concern as to whether it expresses your passion, values, or even fulfills you. This is the approach you find in many business books. I call this the *out-side-in* approach because it starts *outside* of you:

1. Look for a big unsolved problem or desire in the marketplace.

2. Choose products that solve the problem or fulfill the desire.

3. Build or deliver these products to your chosen niche market.

This traditional approach to making money and building companies works. Billions of dollars in profits are made this way. However there is one problem; and unfortunately, this is a major problem.

If you use this old approach, you miss the most important reason you want to be an entrepreneur. Why? You've left out your passion and desire to make a difference.

You've omitted a purpose you are passionate to achieve, one that will motivate both you and your people to achieve the best on a daily basis. You've left out your inner drive to succeed by doing something you enjoy.

Choose a purpose that
motivates you and your team.

Frankly, if your sole reason for owning a business is to make money, you will not remain excited for long. Over time, you will feel empty because you are not inspired by what you are doing. Unless you have a big exciting vision, you will fail to achieve your true profit potential. Worse, your business may falter or even fail.

If there is no deeper purpose to how you make money—if your heart isn't truly in it—then when things get tough or your business feels like a daily grind, you will likely abandon your business and try another.

This is why the Conscious Millionaire approach to making money starts with purpose, the difference you are passionate to create. Then it combines your expansive purpose with a strong competitive advantage to help drive your business for massive growth. I call this the *inside-out* approach because it starts *inside* of you:

1. Discover a visionary difference you are passionate to achieve.

2. Select a market with the problems and desires your vision meets.

3. Provide products that solve their problems and also fulfill their desires.

When you make money this way, you are doing something you are passionate about and believe matters. At the end of the day, you are fulfilled because you know that how you are making money is also serving a bigger purpose. You are creating an important change that helps your customers.

THE 3 WHYS FOR YOUR BUSINESS

Whether you currently have an ongoing business or are planning to start a new business, before you make another decision, determine the three compelling *whys* for your business. These are the three reasons you are choosing to invest your time, resources, and energy in your chosen business. The three *whys* are:

1. Lifestyle Why: To provide the money, options, and free time so you can fully enjoy your ideal life. This is how your business will help you enjoy an abundant lifestyle, provide money to invest for your future, and have the resources to give back to help others.

2. Purpose Why: It's the bigger reason you started your business; the specific transformation your business will help other people, businesses, or organizations achieve. This is how your business helps others and our world become better.

3. End Goal Why: The ultimate financial return you seek by selling, franchising, or taking your business public—how you plan to create a high return on your investment of time, money, and energy to build and grow your business.

The *lifestyle* why is about your personal happiness. The *purpose* why maps out how you and your business will make a difference. Your *end goal* why will determine many of your business decisions, as they must be aligned with your ultimate reasons for owning your business.

*Your three business whys
influence your business model.*

How you answer these three whys is integral to how you will design your business model and make many of your business decisions. Your answers will influence whether you design a business that requires you to work from one location or gives you the freedom to run it virtually. They also influence decisions such as how you staff, design your systems, and fund your business.

The *lifestyle why* is about your personal happiness. If you own a business that doesn't provide you with an opportunity to enjoy your ideal life, you will ultimately resent your business and possibly sabotage its success.

At a minimum, you would likely achieve far less than if you were enjoying your desired life. Therefore, you need to decide how much time off you want, to enjoy family and friends, hobbies, sports, and entertainment.

The *purpose why* is the bigger vision you want your business to accomplish. It is a higher purpose, a greater good of helping others. *This is a purpose that goes beyond making money*. Further, your visionary purpose connects your business with higher consciousness.

Successful entrepreneurs with a visionary purpose include John Mackey, who co-founded WholeFoods to sell health-conscious foods; Oprah Winfrey, who brought meaning to lives through television and radio shows; and the late Steve Jobs, who created Apple and revolutionized both personal computing and how we experience and consume information.

Your *end goal why* is your ultimate end reason, or final outcome, for owning your business. While this may include the difference you want to make, in this section focus on the financial outcome for owning your business.

If you plan to exit your business through a direct sale, then you will select a sale date and maximize cash flow growth. If you want to franchise, then you will focus on efficient systems that can be duplicated and easily taught to others at new locations. If you

> Your visionary purpose connects your business with higher consciousness

want to pass the business to your children, then you will design positions for them so they learn to operate the business and become integral to decision making.

If you want to grow by attracting capital funding, then you will need a professionally written business plan and an experienced management team. You will also need access to external investors and a three to five year exit plan. This usually consists of going public, merging, or being acquired.

> **Coaching:** Open your *Conscious Millionaire Journal*. Write whatever comes into your mind as answers to each of your three *whys*. How, specifically, will your answers influence your approach to designing your business?

How to Transform Your Customer

The purpose of your business is to make an important difference to your customer. While all businesses make some level of difference for their customer, Conscious Millionaire Businesses make a transformational difference. What does this mean?

There are three steps to creating your transformational difference:

1. First, transform your customer by either solving a major problem or providing a means to achieve their dream or aspiration.

2. Second, transform your customer at an even higher level by meeting their emotional needs such as: self-esteem, feeling loved, security, belonging, or happiness.

3. Third, the highest level of transformation occurs when your business changes your customer's life, business, or organization in a way that helps them embody greater *empowerment*, more *competency*, and achieve *mastery*.

As you move up the levels, customers will typically pay more for your products and services. An easy way to think of this is by using dollar signs:

1. **Level One = $**

2. **Level Two = $$**

3. **Level Three = $$$**

The reason you can charge more as you move up the levels of transformation is that you provide a higher value at each level. Now that you know the three levels of transformation, and how the value to your customer increases at each level, you are better prepared in the marketplace.

Your 9 Keys to Conscious Profits

There are nine keys to creating conscious profits. In order to understand what "conscious" means within this context, let's distinguish "ordinary profits" from "conscious profits." In Chapter 1, *Your Millionaire Journey*, we discussed the difference between First Stage Capitalism and Second Stage Capitalism.

In the first stage, there is one primary goal: achieve profits. There is no concern whether products sold have actual intrinsic value or meaningful benefit to customers or society. Moreover, there are no "higher values" or sense of "higher purpose." Profit is the only pursuit.

> Make money by making meaning—that is, by doing something that creates a difference, helps others, and improves the world.

By contrast, *Second Stage Capitalism* focuses on value provided to all those concerned—which includes each of the seven stakeholders. *Note*: increasingly businesses are considering their impact on the environment because they realize we all depend on a healthy planet for survival.

In *Second Stage Capitalism*, there are two *primary goals*: to achieve both *higher purpose* and *higher profit*. Put in other terms, to make money by making meaning—that is, by doing something that creates a difference, helps others, and improves the world.

Moreover, it is by combining these two goals with higher level values, such as honesty and integrity, that one creates conscious profits. Conscious Millionaire is a *Second Stage Capitalism* approach and movement.

The nine keys for developing conscious profits is the business model I teach entrepreneurs. These are equally important for start-ups and ongoing businesses. Here are the nine keys:

1. Your Purpose/Values: Your visionary purpose is *why* you are in business. It sets the direction in which your business is headed. For a purpose to lead to higher profits, it must be big and expansive. While this may sound lofty, the truth is, such visions come from reaching into higher consciousness. A visionary purpose conveys a possible future that is positively charged and emotionally important to your team, prospects, and customers. It communicates a vision of how you will *transform* others and help them in ways that are meaningful and valuable to them.

Every company that achieves enduring greatness has a purpose that improves lives by accomplishing something that goes beyond only making money. A great purpose touches you and all those involved in your business so deeply that it makes you each feel excited and motivated to see it accomplished.

It's important at the outset of discussing the nine keys to conscious profits to define the actual relationship between your *purpose* and your *profit* motive. This is an area in which there is often a great deal of confusion. However, the relationship is very simple to define and easy to understand. It is obvious because it makes good business sense.

The reason you are in business is neither to deliver on your purpose nor to achieve a profit—that is, the reason is not one or the other, it is *both*. By delivering on your purpose, your business attracts more prospects, closes more sales, and can generate more profits. Likewise, by creating more profits, you are able to expand your business, serve more customers, and thereby make a larger difference. Your two reasons for being in business, to deliver your purpose and make a profit, are inextricably intertwined. They complement and strengthen one another.

Shifting to discuss your core values, these are your top three to five values that are important in your business. While values are your ideals and higher aspirations, thinking of them this way can make them feel ethereal and hard to grasp. However, by defining values in terms of specific behaviors or results that are high priorities for your business, they are often easier to understand.

> Your two reasons for being in business, to deliver your purpose and make a profit, are inextricably intertwined.

Your values convey what is important at the core of your business. They express how you want to do business, achieve your purpose, and make money. Both your purpose and values emanate from the core of your model and infuse every aspect of your business.

2. Your Brand Promise: This is your commitment to your customers that you will consistently keep. It is a promise which will inform every marketing decision and execution, the development and delivery of each product and service you offer, and all touch points your customers have with your business. It is an expectation that you create in the mind of your customer about what they will experience each time they interact with your business.

Think of your brand promise as why customers continually come back. It's what attracts them to your brand rather than your competitors. When your brand promise is both clear and effectively delivered, it is why customers go beyond merely liking you, to becoming raving fans who are the true evangelists for your business.

> Your brand should create a clear mental picture, deep emotional feeling, and visceral sensation in your ideal customer.

Developing your brand promise requires you to identify the factors that define how your brand is different from your major competitors. Develop a short list of important factors. These are your brand *differentiators*. Then think about the top two to three benefits that your customers most value about doing business with you. These are your brand *benefits*. Your top benefits should help your ideal customer either remove their pains or achieve their aspirations.

Finally, consider how your brand will create a deep sensory experience that is memorable. This is your *brand memory*. Your brand should create a clear mental picture, deep emotional feeling, and visceral sensation in your ideal customer—one that creates a lasting positive association with your business. This association should evoke a desire in customers to buy more and tell others about your brand.

3. Your Financial Goals: You achieve what you focus on in both business and life. Therefore, if you want to rapidly grow your business and achieve your visionary purpose, then constantly increase your revenues and profits. In order to generate rapid growth, you need to set financial goals that challenge, stretch, and require everyone to perform at their highest levels. This means both you and everyone connected with your business strive to develop the best products and services, then provide the highest quality customer service.

Your financial goals influence numerous decisions you will make about your business and business model. *For example*: There must be enough customers in your niche market that selling to only a small percentage of your market will support you in realizing your financial goals. In addition, the customers must have the money or access to credit so they can afford to purchase your products and services at your targeted price points.

If you have weak revenue and profits, you will at best flounder; at worst, go out of business. However, when you have growing revenues and profits, you can expand your business, touch more lives, and make a bigger difference in our world. In order to achieve your targets, utilize financial *metrics* to measure your results. These include: the *cost* to acquire each customer; the *speed* with which you acquire each customer; and your *breakeven* day—that is the point you move from losses to profits for the month.

4. Your Market Niche: In order to develop a strong customer base, select one well-defined market niche. As you collect more information on your niche through their responses to your marketing and through interactions with customers, you will become aware that what once appeared to be one niche can actually be subdivided into numerous "micro-niches." Each micro-niche has its own specific characteristics, favorite words, activities it enjoys, and way in which those who comprise it respond to marketing messages. The more you know about each micro-niche, the more you can tailor your message and products to their specific desires and needs.

Think of your market as
having 100 or more micro-niches.

There are four aspects to selecting market niches. *First*, each market niche must *passionately desire* what you are selling. *Second*, it must have the *money*, which may include access to credit, so it can buy what you are selling at a price point that supports your financial goal. *Third*, each market niche must be large enough so even having a small percentage of it will allow you to achieve your targeted profits, now and in future years. In marketing terms, this means you have a deep niche.

And *fourth*, each of your market niches must be narrowly defined rather than a broad, general group. In summary: Each market niche must be comprised of people who are passionate about your brand, have the money to buy, is a group large enough to support your desired profits, and can be narrowly defined.

Understanding your market and the people within it is an endless journey of discovering how they think, feel, and act. It is a journey of getting inside their heads, hearts, and very souls so you can experience life as if you were them. It requires knowing where they live, with whom they associate, their passions, sense of purpose, and deeply held values. It is a journey of understanding the specific problems they are eager to solve now, their emotional wounds that need healing, and their unmet dreams. It is a journey of developing a deep connection with your market.

5. Your Products: Think of "products" as including what are traditional products, as well as services and experiences (such as theme parks). To create high profits, your products must meet three criteria:

• First, your products create a transformational difference for your customers by: eliminating their pain or helping them achieve dreams; meeting their emotional needs; and helping them become empowered, create competency, and achieve mastery.

• Second, your products must give you big *profit margins*. Without big profit margins (the difference between what you charge and your direct product costs), you will find it difficult to achieve high profits that propel growth.

• Third, provide your products in the specific way your customers prefer. *For example*: boxed, digital, hard copy, bright colors, delivered overnight, a three-week course instead of six weeks, or anything else your customers desire.

As you will learn in the next chapter, the most profitable way to develop a product is to: understand your customer; seek their feedback as you develop your product; and test the price at which they will purchase to assure you will have a big profit margin.

6. Your Marketing: Consider marketing as everything you do to attract the attention of the ideal prospect in your niche market; emotionally connect with your prospect; and stimulate their desire to buy from you. In considering any marketing action, you should always ask three questions:

1. What specific *result* is a marketing action designed to accomplish?

2. Can this action be *tracked* as being the actual cause of that result?

3. Can the result be *measured*?

Unless you can answer "yes" to all three of these questions, you have no method to determine the real return you receive on each marketing dollar. I suggest that 80 percent to 90 percent of your marketing budget be allocated to marketing tactics (actions) that allow you to track and measure results. Even those few marketing activities not easy to track and measure should be designed to attract customers and lead to sales.

Examples of activities that are often harder to track include: advertising, public relations, sponsorships, and some aspects of social and mobile media.

7. Your Selling: Think of selling as the process, or steps, necessary to convert prospects into happy buying customers. Selling begins by connecting with a prospect who has self-identified themselves as interested (the result of marketing), and continues by guiding them through steps that lead to their purchase decision. Conscious Millionaire selling involves more than just closing a sale. It also includes evaluating what is actually *right for a prospect.*

A higher-consciousness approach to selling includes always being mindful of what is in the customers' best interest, both in terms of the product you offer and the price. When you make additional offers to your customers, it isn't to "separate them from their wallets," as lower-conscious sellers often try to accomplish. It is to provide customers with *additional value* that

> A higher-consciousness approach to selling includes always being mindful of what is in the customers' best interest.

you believe, and feel in your heart, will benefit them. Over the long term, your brand will grow the most and attain the highest profit levels by consciously focusing on what will honestly benefit your customers.

8. Your Rules and Systems: Your rules provide a context in which your business can operate. They provide your team members with a structure that allows them to effectively work together, make good decisions, and achieve your goals. Without rules, all the stakeholders, including your team members, suppliers, and even customers, would make up their own rules. And this would result in total chaos and eventual collapse.

However, when you consciously develop and fully communicate rules, you make it possible for your business to achieve its purpose, benefit stakeholders, and create profits. This is because your rules incorporate your purpose, values, and priorities. They inform your business culture and communicate how you do business to your team, customers, suppliers, and community in which you live or work.

Because you have rules, it is possible for you to develop systems. Each of your systems consists of a sequence of steps designed to achieve a specific outcome. In general, a system begins with the first step, referred to as the *input*, and continues step after step, until the completion of the last step, referred to as the *output*.

In your business, automate as many of your systems as possible because this allows you to scale rapidly through easy duplication of activities. Whether manual or automated, your systems should be both efficient (have the least number of steps) and effective (achieve the exact result you desire). This will reduce expenses and contribute to profitable growth.

One of the greatest values that systems provide your business is *scalability*. This refers to the ability of a system to expand and adapt to increased demands without having to undergo major changes. When constructing your business model, consider other aspects of scalability, such as your ability to rapidly increase product production. Also, utilize systems to automate your marketing and selling so that you can acquire more customers, make a bigger difference, and generate greater sales.

Consider how well your systems allow for the efficient training of new people. In addition, your systems should also permit you to rapidly duplicate your business, which adds to your scalability. *For example*: Systems allow you to open new locations for your business as well as create franchises by selling a duplicate of your systemized business model.

9. Your "Give Back:" Giving back to your community and causes you believe in is not only the right thing to do, it is also good business. It extends the reach of your business purpose by also choosing to transform your community. When you give back in a way that is fully consistent with your business purpose and core values, the choices you make around your giving will help create an emotional bond with your ideal prospects and customers.

This is because the type of causes that mean the most to you will likely also resonate with your prospects and customers. Moreover, when you and your team personally volunteer to help with a cause, you raise awareness of your business. Through your involvement, you may also build new connections that could result in additional prospects, strategic partners, and business opportunities. If giving

> Giving back to your community and causes you believe in is not only the right thing to do, it is also good business.

back is new for your business, begin by choosing one cause or community project; donate a percentage of your profits, such as two percent to five percent; and volunteer as a team to help with the cause or project.

Conscious Millionaire businesses do more than make money. They also make an important difference. This is why as a Conscious Millionaire entrepreneur you serve as a role model for your customers, other businesses, and your community.

> **Coaching:** Open your *Conscious Millionaire Journal*. Using the information contained in the "Your Brand Promise" section, create your brand promise. How does it differentiate your business from other businesses in your market?

Conscious Millionaire Business Model

Utilize the *Conscious Millionaire Business Model* as the blueprint for developing your own business model. Even if you have been in business for years, it's always good to take a fresh look at your business. You can always discover new ways to create greater growth, a greater difference, and greater profits.

In the center of this model are your purpose/values and brand promise. Think of them as radiating out in all directions. Located directly on the circle are your market niche, products, financial goals, and give back program.

Connecting your market niche to products is your marketing. This consists of the actions necessary to attract your prospect's attention, gain their interest, and move them toward your product. Connecting products to profit is selling. It includes the actions required to sell a new prospect or existing customer— to close the sale. Next, put the money from sales in the bank, which helps you achieve your financial goals.

Because you utilize a portion of your profits (and resources, which may include your team) to give back, an arrow connects your financial goals to give back. Finally, because your give back involvement helps you develop business, both by increasing awareness of your business and connecting with new prospects and strategic partners, an arrow connects give back to market niche.

Notice that market niche, products, financial goals, and give back are continuously connected in a flow of activities that move in a never-ending clockwise direction.

Encircling the model are your rules and systems as well as financial metrics. Your rules provide a context and structure for doing business. Your systems are how you achieve each of your task-related results. Your metrics monitor how well you are achieving your financial goals.

Why is your business model so important? It's the very foundation for building your business. It pains me to tell you how many good people there are (and you may know people like this) who are hard-working entrepreneurs who desire to make a difference. Yet, instead of making a big difference and impact, they end up failing in business. Worse, some of them wind up broke or even bankrupt.

They love what they do, care about others, and genuinely want to make this a better world. Yet, they don't have the right business model.

Doing what you love
can ONLY make you rich,
IF you have the right business model!

To turn your business model into profitable growth, you also need a one-year success plan and the motivation to execute and achieve rapid growth. You will develop both in Chapter 14, *Create Your Millionaire Plan*!

Coaching: Open your *Conscious Millionaire Journal*. Use the nine keys to conscious profits to create your own business model. Consider your model to be a work in progress, one that will undergo many *iterations*, or versions, as you grow your business.

Conscious Focused Action Model

This is the twelfth version of the foundational model, which is found in Chapter 2, *Formula for Creating Wealth*.

The two tiers of the conscious level are interrelated; utilize each of the *keys to conscious profits* on the top tier with each of words the on the bottom tier. *For example*: Utilizing "brand promise" from the top tier, ask:

CONSCIOUS FOCUSED ACTION MODEL - 12

• "What result will the *brand promise* help achieve?" and, "Why is using the *brand promise* to accomplish this result a priority?"

• "Who will benefit from using the *brand promise* to achieve this result?" and, "Who will help use the *brand promise* to attain this result?"

• "How can I best utilize this *brand promise* to reach this result?"

Note: The brand promise will benefit customers. Who else will it benefit?

The focus level changes to include the seven stakeholders. These are organized within the three conscious perspectives: *yourself* (owner-entrepreneurs and investors/lenders), *others* (customers, team, and suppliers), and *society* (community and environment).

The conscious level and focus level interrelate by asking how each of the nine conscious profit keys benefits each of the seven stakeholders.

Approach the other three levels—action, result, and learning—the same as in the foundational model. If you don't fully achieve your desired result, want to improve your process, or care to achieve your result at a higher level, then iterate. Review each level to determine what needs to change. Return to the conscious level and make the changes as you go through the model again. Then *test* the changes to determine if they are actually better.

CONSCIOUS MILLIONAIRE COACHING

Build Your Strategy

Open your *Conscious Millionaire Journal*. Write a three-step business strategy using *conscious focused action*. Develop your strategy utilizing the concept provided in the *conscious* step below. It is an important concept from this chapter.

1. Conscious: Consider the importance of transforming your customer. Develop a goal to achieve this at the highest levels. *For example*: "Each month our team meets to identify one specific way to improve an existing approach or create a new way to transform our customers."

2. Focused: As you focus on your goal, choose three actions that will help you begin to achieve it. Determine the precise order for your actions.

3. Action: During the next twenty-four hours, execute by taking your three actions.

Grow Your Business

In your *Conscious Millionaire Journal* make notes on how you utilize each of the following to grow your business:

• Determine your "exit why" for building your business. If it is to sell, choose a target price and date on which you want to sell your business.

• Select one of the keys to conscious profits. Develop as many ideas as you can for how to use that key to grow your business.

• Identify an *additional* customer market you could help; then select one of your existing products or services to sell them.

Create Your Journey

Here are three choices for what to read next. The first is to read another *conscious* section. The second is to read another *millionaire* section. The third choice is to *journey* through the book linearly, reading it chapter by chapter.

 Conscious: You may want to review "The New Entrepreneur Path" section in Chapter 1, *Your Millionaire Journey*, before continuing to the next chapter.

 Millionaire: Take a look at "Your One Year Success Plan" section in Chapter 14, *Create Your Millionaire Plan*, before going to the next chapter.

 Journey: Continue forward to Chapter 13, *Prepare for Fast Growth*.

QR Codes / Links

 Go to the membership site and view a coaching video that presents an example of how to create your *Conscious Millionaire Business Model*. As an added bonus, download a blank copy of the model to utilize in creating your own business model. Access the site now at: **ConsciousMillionaire.com/member**

PREPARE FOR
FAST GROWTH

*Rapid growth results
from your being fully prepared.*

In this chapter, you discover how to achieve rapid success by constantly iterating your business model. You will learn how to define your customer avatar. You also discover how to create high-demand products, ones your customers eagerly buy because they provide great value. Then you learn the Conscious Millionaire approach to marketing and sales as well as how marketing systems help you achieve fast growth. Lastly, you will utilize the *Conscious Focused Action Model* to move forward on your Conscious Millionaire Journey.

HOW TO ACHIEVE SUCCESS QUICKLY

In 1927, Walt Disney created a cartoon character named, "Oswald the Lucky Rabbit." However, there was a problem.

Disney Brother Studios was owned by Universal Pictures and Disney was fired. So, he started a new company and created a new character, which his wife named, "Mickey Mouse." The first version had bulky eyes, skinny legs, and no gloves.

Mickey's first cartoon was a silent film which was made in 1928. However, no distributor wanted the film, so it was never shown in theaters. Walt decided to forge ahead, and made more changes, including releasing Mickey in a seven-minute black and white cartoon that had sound. The name of Mickey's first cartoon to be seen in theaters was "Steamboat Willie."

Through numerous *iterations* (changes and refinements), Mickey evolved into the beloved mascot of the Disney brand. Not only did his appearance change, including the addition of his trademark big, white gloves, so did his role.

Mickey evolved from a black and white, short cartoon character into a feature-length movie star in the film "Fantasia." His role continued to expand into comics, video games, and into being an action-hero figure.

Although Mickey became a huge success, initially no distributor was interested in him. Through perseverance and a commitment to develop his successful cartoon figure, Walt Disney evolved his mouse into the iconic figure that helped the Disney companies become highly profitable. There is a moral to this story and it reveals an important business secret.

> Your business model will never be "perfect." You will always be changing and improving it as you advance forward.

Your journey to success will take a similar path. Initial models and early ideas about your business will likely contain many errors and incorrect assumptions. Your business model may require numerous iterations for your business to become a big success.

By utilizing the *Conscious Focused Action Model* and making changes based upon what works, and doesn't, you will rapidly develop a business model that supports long-term growth. Your business model will never be "perfect." You will always be changing and improving it as you advance forward.

You will continually iterate every aspect of your business model. This includes constantly studying your customers' most painful problems as well as their biggest dreams.

You will discover which products sell at what prices and how to deliver them in ways that delight your customers. You will learn what *actually* works in marketing and sales, not what you currently *assume* will work.

> *Rapid success results*
> *from executing quickly!*

Everything about your business will constantly change as you test what you think would work against what truly works. And, whether you currently own a business or are starting a new business, you only have two choices:

1. Spend the next year *building your business* on paper, imagining what your customer might want, dreaming of the products you will create, and building a *grand illusion* of all the profits you may someday make; or

2. Spend the next year *building your business* in reality by rapidly creating a business model and success plan, then executing to *achieve escape velocity*. How? By consciously focusing your actions in one direction until you achieve the growth level you desire.

Take *conscious focused action* and make the necessary changes to move your business forward. As you discover what works, focus all of your energy on doing it.

Where will you be in twelve months? More importantly, where will you be in *seven* days? Will you still be building an imaginary company, working hard to design the perfect business model, *or* will you have created an initial, "bare bones" model, and be executing to create profits? How—by quickly making changes as you discover what works.

DEVELOP A GROWTH CULTURE

Think of your culture as the environment in which your business operates. This environment expresses the very consciousness, or essence, of your business. It encompasses the range of behaviors that are expected and accepted within your business—the rules by which you operate. These are influenced by your shared purpose, values, goals, beliefs, and unique company rituals.

> It is only through raising the consciousness of each team member that your business can consciously operate and grow.

Conscious leadership is at the center of developing a growth culture that supports your Conscious Millionaire business. It is only through the constant evolution of your own consciousness, as both the owner and leader of your business, that you can develop a growth culture.

Everything that you say, each action you take, and every decision you make, communicates what is, and what is not expected and accepted in your business.

As the leader of your business, your choices include both the people you select to be on your team and how you develop them. This will determine whether your business germinates a growth culture.

As you develop your culture, consider the three growth areas for your business: the growth of your *business* itself; the growth and empowerment of each *individual* team member; and the growth of your *team as whole.*

Your business growth involves the *dual focus* of expanding how you bring forth your purpose and grow your profits. A growth culture supports the transformation of your customers and the uplifting of humanity.

Exude a conscious energy daily in how you think, feel, and act in your business. Further, invite everyone involved in your business to make decisions and take *conscious focused actions* designed to achieve profitable growth—both short-term and long-term.

To create a growth culture, place a high priority on the constant growth, learning, and advancement of your people. This goes beyond skill-based training to include the personal growth and conscious development of each person on your team. It is only through raising the consciousness of each team member that your business can consciously operate and grow.

However, it isn't sufficient to focus solely on individual growth; create a culture that also supports your team's growth as a whole. This includes a culture in which mutual support, mutual respect, and mutual rewards are a way of life.

Further, it is imperative that you implement all seven relationship keys discussed in the "Conscious Relationships in Business" section in Chapter 10, *Build Powerful Relationships*. As your people grow, your business naturally grows as well.

> **Coaching:** Open your *Conscious Millionaire Journal*. Develop a list of five to ten actions that would support the personal growth and conscious development of each team member. If you are a solo-preneur, then focus the list on actions you can take to support your growth and development.

Build Your Customer Avatar

If you want to become financially successful, one of your top priorities must be to build an *accurate* picture of your ideal customer. This is often referred to as your customer *avatar*: the thoughts, feelings, actions, interests, problems, aspirations and concerns of your ideal customer. And, in order to fully understand your customer, you must take a journey into *their world*.

As you take a journey into your customer's world, ask yourself how you can help raise their consciousness. How can you both inspire and support them in moving to a higher state of awareness and mindfulness about their problems, aspirations, and emotional needs. Consider what is missing in their lives that is keeping them from transforming to a higher level of living, operating their business, or expressing the purpose of their organization.

To do this, you need to connect with them in a way that opens your customers to share their innermost thoughts and feelings with you. If you want to connect at this level, then show them true respect and regard as a person.

This requires you to utilize your tonality, word choice, and body language in a way that communicates your genuine care for them. It can't be faked. It must be authentic and real. It must be true for you and your entire team. It must be your actual intention, because if it isn't, your relationship will end before it ever begins.

In order to build an avatar, determine what motivates your customers at the deepest levels. This includes motivations such as achieving self-esteem, attaining wealth, or improving the ways in which they want to see themselves and are viewed by others. What is the chatter that goes on in their minds (their self-talk) when they are thinking about what they want and how they feel?

> As you take a journey into your customer's world, ask yourself how you can help raise their consciousness.

You also need to know what your customers fear as well as understand their deepest emotional wounds. Become aware of what they enjoy, like, dislike, love and hate. Know their hobbies and why they choose them.

It is necessary for you to discover their grandest hopes, dreams and desires that are unrequited. What is missing in their lives; in what ways are they unfulfilled?

Most importantly, discover *their major problems* and *deepest pains*. Remember major is in *their eyes*, not yours. If it is major to them, they are eager to solve it. This makes it a primary reason they will buy your product or service.

The key question: what are *they actively seeking* right now? Is it a solution to that major annoying problem? Is it a way to experience that unfulfilled hope, dream or desire? Or is it a way to increase their self worth? *For example*: To heighten their sense of status, lose weight, or feel more beautiful? Whatever it is, this will motivate them to buy and buy *now*—if you provide them with a solution for attaining this outcome.

Building your customer avatar is actually a journey that never ends. This is because there are always fresh nuances you can develop as you refine your picture. Your customers are always *evolving*. They grow, change, and interact with the world in new ways, not only as their own lives shift, but as technology and society shift as well.

In your quest to build your customer avatar, consider three ways to gather information and develop an understanding of your customer:

1. Reports or surveys that others conduct;

2. Surveys you conduct online, by phone, or in person; or

3. Your ongoing interactions with prospects and customers.

I suggest you review any reports or surveys you can find. However, your best information often comes from your own work. In terms of conducting surveys, you can easily discover free or low-cost options on the Internet. Develop or obtain lists that contain your type of customer, then call them to conduct a phone survey.

> *To create fast profit growth,*
> *you must understand your customer.*

What is most important when you survey is to discover two pieces of information. First, determine the problem they want solved, or the dream they want to achieve—right now. This is the overall problem to which they are actively seeking a solution. Second, discover how they feel about it. Although you can ask about their feelings in an online or paper survey, the best way to discover their emotions is on the phone or, even better, in person.

You will usually receive your most complete information from in-person, face-to-face, conversations. In this type of situation, you can connect deeper and easily develop trust. And, with trust comes more openness.

Being face-to-face will help the person you are interviewing feel more comfortable. They will reveal the deeper aspects of who they are, including their intimate thoughts and feelings. You will also obtain more information through their facial expressions and overall body language.

Coaching: Open your *Conscious Millionaire Journal*. Develop a list of five to ten open-ended survey questions. Choose one method (in-person, phone, Internet survey) for surveying prospects or customers. Then survey at least 20 customers or prospects. Utilize what you learn to create your first version of your customer avatar.

CREATE HIGH-DEMAND PRODUCTS

Think of a "product" as anything you can sell your customer; this includes traditional products as well as services. The first step in developing high-demand products, the ones your customers will eagerly buy, is to build your customer avatar. This includes creating a detailed picture of their pressing problems and aspirations—and their hot-button feelings about them.

Once you understand these, focus your attention on developing ideas for how to achieve your visionary business purpose. These include transforming your customers' life, business, or organization.

Until you have a deep understanding of your ideal customers' problems and aspirations, and have created potential answers that could help them, any attempt to build a product is a waste of time. Why? Because you would only be guessing at what your customers might buy.

> As an entrepreneur, it is your responsibility to craft a product that solves customers' problems or helps them achieve their dreams.

As an entrepreneur, it is *your* responsibility to craft a product that solves customers' problems or helps them achieve their dreams. You accomplish this by taking what your customers have revealed to you and the potential answers you develop, then using them to create ideas for potential products.

Model other top-selling products. Start with what they are doing that appears to be working. Then add your content and transformational process. Obtain your ideal customers' input as you create your product. Survey and iterate.

Here's how to do this in 9 steps:

1. Survey your ideal customers to develop an initial understanding of the problems they *actively* seek to solve and aspirations they actively seek to achieve

(strong motivation). Expand this to include the upper two levels of customer transformation: meeting emotional needs and helping them achieve empowerment, competency, and mastery.

2. Determine the "hot button" for each problem and aspiration (the foundational level of customer transformation.) Recall that a hot button is a high intensity emotion associated with pain customers want to avoid or pleasure they seek to experience.

3. Choose one (or more) of your customers' problems/aspirations as the basic reason for creating the product. At a minimum, the product *must* solve these problems/aspirations. That is what makes it valuable—it is why the customer will purchase it.

4. Research to identify other products in the marketplace that address these same problems/aspirations. If the purpose of the product is to also reach into the upper two levels of customer transformation, look for products that achieve these outcomes as well. Evaluate which products are selling, at what prices. Also determine the features and benefits of top-selling products. *Note*: The benefit is always from the customers' perspective.

5. Develop ideas for several potential products you could create that would solve the problem/aspiration (or combination of problems/aspirations) that you chose. Select *one* product to develop.

6. Make a basic product model based upon what you know about your prospects or customers (and if it is a service, design the basic, introductory service).

7. While providing prospects and customers an experience of the initial product or service, survey them to determine if this is something they would buy. Record their responses and either start over (if you are completely off the mark) or refine the current product to align it more closely with your customers' vision of what they desire.

8. Using steps six and seven. Add features each time you present the product or service model to your customers—to make it more valuable.

9. Finally, test prices. Your goal is to determine the price that will provide the highest gross profit in a specific period of time. The formula is simple:

$$units\ sold \times gross\ profit/unit = total\ gross\ profit$$

The only way to discover this is to offer your product, online or offline, through split-tested pricing (offering the same product at two prices). Continue to split test, noting at each iteration, which of the two prices yielded the highest total gross profit. Within two to three iterations, you will likely discover the price your market wants to pay for your product.

Once you have a product and price, your next step is to develop a process for marketing your product.

Coaching: Open your *Conscious Millionaire Journal.* Utilize the information in this section to outline how you will develop a product your customers will eagerly buy. Consider including all three levels of customer transformation as goals for how your product will benefit your customers.

Conscious Marketing and Selling

The unfortunate reality is that up to 90 percent of business owners cease to be in business within the first five years, and most of the remaining 10 percent never make a big difference or achieve big profits. In fact, many of the businesses that make it past five years, just end up struggling or stagnating. They never achieve true *escape velocity*. What does this mean? Escape velocity means *doubling* your business every one to three years.

If you want to build a highly-profitable, successful business, then focus on becoming one of the *top three percent*—the businesses that grow rapidly, excel, and change their customers and our world. They put themselves in the position to make an important difference by growing and expanding their capacity to help others.

> *The #1 reason businesses fail*
> *is they don't have enough customers!*

If you want to achieve fast growth, you need to become skilled at acquiring customers. You have no other option. However, the approach you utilize to obtain your customers will determine not only the profits you make, but, also, the difference you make. Further, it will determine whether you maintain high ethics and conscious values, such as honesty and integrity.

Increasingly, many businesses that utilize traditional approaches to marketing and selling are finding that these old, often manipulative tactics, are no longer as effective as they once were. Why is this occurring?

Because customers are becoming more conscious. They are waking up. They are becoming aware of the difference between "being sold" and "being cared for" as a customer and as a human being. Increasingly, they want the latter.

As the new Conscious Millionaire entrepreneur, you have a true advantage in today's marketplace. Why? You care. You seek to make a difference and provide exceptional value. You want to meet the needs of your customer through conscious marketing, selling, and business practices. Increasingly, this is what the marketplace wants as well.

Now, consider the approaches to value exchange which we discussed in the "Mindset of Highly-Successful Entrepreneurs" section of Chapter 8, *Create an Abundance Mindset*. Recall the entrepreneur type who only cares about themselves, always wants the "benefit of the bargain," and constantly seeks to obtain far more value then they deliver.

This is the business philosophy of many *First Stage Capitalism* entrepreneurs. "What is in it for me?" not "How can I best serve and benefit others?" is often their battle cry. This philosophy not only shows up in *how* they market, but in the *language* they use to describe their marketing.

For example: they want to "hook the customer," "exploit emotional wounds," and "maximize sales at all costs." By contrast, as a Conscious Millionaire entrepreneur you want to "attract your ideal customer" by offering something that matters to them; "meet emotional needs" by helping your customers; and maximize sales by "adding greater value."

Entrepreneurs who maintain the *First Stage Capitalism* view, only think of sales in terms of their own profits. At most they give lip service to helping their clients. They see profit, at any cost, as the only purpose of business. And, we all know what it feels like to be sold to in this way.

By contrast, as a Conscious Millionaire entrepreneur, you embrace *Second Stage Capitalism*. You realize that there is a better way—a way in which you as the business owner can achieve higher profits by bringing greater value to your customers and our world. You believe in the *Triple Win*: you, others, and society *all winning together*.

The Conscious Millionaire approach infuses every aspect of marketing and selling with higher consciousness. This includes a mindfulness that when you close a sale, you are not only being of service to your customers, but to the world as well. Moreover, each sale you close is an opportunity to express your purpose, an opportunity to make your difference.

You make your difference by serving and transforming your customers so that they enjoy their lives more, operate their businesses at a higher level, or express the purpose of their organizations more fully.

In order to accomplish this honorable goal, you must become an expert at closing sales—with heart, integrity, and a desire to help others. Selling must become your passion. Allow yourself to now let go of any negative views you once held about selling. Replace them with the positive view that selling is helping others fulfill their needs and desires.

Marketing begins with attracting a prospect's attention and continues with developing a relationship with them. Selling begins when someone self-identifies as a prospect who is interested in your offer. Selling continues through however many contacts and actions are necessary for your prospect to make a purchase; for you to help them and close the sale.

In summary, although marketing and sales are two distinct processes, together they serve your *dual focus* as a Conscious Millionaire business: achieve a *higher purpose* and create *higher profits*. In the next section you will discover how to develop your marketing-sales system.

Coaching: Open your *Conscious Millionaire Journal*. Describe three ways you can utilize a conscious approach to marketing and sales to grow your business. How does each give you an advantage in the marketplace?

The Power of Marketing Systems

A system is a sequence of steps designed to achieve a specific outcome. By developing a system for how you market and sell, you have a repeatable, step-by-step approach for consistently attracting prospects and closing sales. By utilizing a system, you can help more people; generate more revenue; and make a bigger difference.

The goal of all marketing systems is to both be *efficient* (have the least number of steps, or stages, necessary) and *effective* (achieve the exact marketing and sales goals desired). One of the greatest values of a marketing-selling system is *scalability*. This refers to the ability of the system to expand and adapt to increased demands without undergoing major changes.

In order to create a successful marketing system, first identify either a problem that customers want to solve or a dream/aspiration they deeply yearn to achieve. This must be something they are *actively* seeking—right now.

Think of this as their *hot button*. The *content* (problem or aspiration) is the first part of the button; the *emotion* is the second part of the button. The emotion is what makes the button *HOT*.

When you discover a *hot button*, you have a *motivated* prospect. Once you identify the *hot button* and have developed a *product* you know your customer wants and will help them, you are ready to design your system to *attract* your prospect and then close the sale.

Consider marketing and selling as an integrated system. The following diagram describes the *five stages* you will want to develop in your marketing-sales system. Whether you *automate* most of your marketing and selling, by using software that executes the steps automatically, or utilize people to perform each of the stages, your system will help you rapidly grow your business—your system helps you scale.

Five Stage Marketing-Sales System

Stage 1	Stage 2	Stage 3	Stage 4	Stage 5
Attract Engage	Conversation Relationship	First Purchase	Referral Testimonial	Lifetime Purchases

Stage One: Your *first stage* is "attract and engage." Attract your prospect's attention in ways that engage them. Do this by asking a question that includes their problem and the emotion they have about it. *For example*: "Is it a hassle for you to find the time to get your car washed?"

Next, engage them. You could relate a story about yourself or one of your customers with their same problem: "I understand. Many of my clients use me because their schedules are too busy to be waiting around at a car wash."

Stage Two: After you attract and engage them, begin the *second stage*, which is "conversation and relationship." In this stage, you begin what is an ongoing process of building a relationship with your prospect. You talk to people all the time. This is no different. Ask your prospects open-ended questions about their interests, problems, aspirations— and how they *feel* about these.

> Use your prospect's words and frames of reference. Participate in the conversation they are already having in their own mind

Let them talk. You listen. Guide the conversation with questions that probe their problem of having a dirty car. Learn how they feel about being too busy to get it washed. Discover what they say to themselves about this problem. What is their internal chatter?

Once you know this, enter their conversation; use your prospect's words and frames of reference. Participate in the conversation they are already having in their own mind. Then authentically, with the integrity and a desire to help them, provide a solution that is best for their situation.

Develop a relationship by continuing to listen, and occasionally talk. Remember to focus on *them*. It is their problem that is being solved or dream that is being fulfilled, not yours. Your role is to facilitate that solution—naturally, easily, and enjoyably. As you discuss your product, realize you are providing a solution that will help them—that you are serving them.

Stage Three: Now, you are ready for *stage three*, providing them with an opportunity that will help them. This is the how to help your prospect make their "first purchase." Offer them the benefits of your solution. Focus on how your solution resolves any negative feelings they have. Build a sensory rich picture of how your solution will help them transition to the positive feelings they seek to experience.

For example: say something like, "Based on what you've told me about your dirty car, and all the hassles and inconvenience you've had trying to keep it clean, I suggest you consider my car wash services. We come to your house or office, whenever it is convenient for you, and we have packages to fit anyone's budget, from basic wash to full detail."

Most importantly, ask for the sale. Inquire as to how they would like to pay for their car wash. Offer a multiple wash option that saves them money. *Asking* is how you close the sale. Then accept the money and thank them. Also notice that both you and your customer win—by winning together.

Stage Four: While many people hesitate at this point, the most natural thing to do is to move into *stage four*, "referral and testimonial." Ask for one to three referrals. After all, you want to help more people, and a referral is the most effective and easiest way to do that.

Then ask for a testimonial about how you helped them and how excited they are about their purchase. Invite them to describe why they made the purchase and how they believe it will improve their situation.

For example: you could say something like, "I'm really trying to get the word out about this mobile time-saving car wash system. Do you know of anyone else who might want this? What would you say to them, to encourage them to try it out? That sounds great! Would you write that down on this paper and allow me to use it to help others? Thanks. I really appreciate your help."

Stage Five: The real financial value to your business of each customer is NOT their first purchase. If you break-even and make no profit on the initial sale, this can still be a very profitable business strategy. How? The reason is found in *stage five*, "lifetime purchases."

> Connect with each prospect and customer authentically. Engage them in a way that is real and genuine.

If you build a relationship with an ideal customer, then your business will be rewarded many times over—as will your new customer—by all the value and assistance your business will provide for them over the coming years!

To review: Marketing is a step-by-step process of letting your customer know about your product offer and helping them understand how it can help them. Selling is the step-by-step process of helping them buy your product so they can use it and get the benefits they are seeking.

Once you make an initial sale, continue to build your relationship with your customer. *For example*: you may provide information that is useful to your customer, offer free trainings on how to utilize your products, or maintain your relationship through ongoing personal contact.

As new products become available that could help your customer, use the same process: attract their attention, deepen your relationship, offer them value—and close another sale. Then request additional referrals and obtain new testimonials.

The goal of your marketing and sales system is to help you build a long-term, mutually-beneficial relationship with each customer. Think of marketing and selling in this way and you will become emotionally comfortable at each stage of the process.

Notice that I didn't mention whether this sale occurred offline or online. The reason is simple. You can use the above process to make a sale in person, on the phone, or on the Internet. The five stages are the same, whether you market online or offline.

We have already discussed the #1 reason most businesses go out of business—they don't have enough customers. Now, I want to reveal the #1 secret to long-term marketing and sales success. The secret is to be *authentic*—to express genuine care and concern for the best interests of your customer.

Go inside yourself and find that place where deep authenticity and genuineness resides. Design your marketing and sales process with the "conscious intent" of always being authentic. Then, connect with each prospect and customer authentically. Engage them in a way that is real and genuine. Connect with them person-to-person.

Coaching: Open your *Conscious Millionaire Journal*. Create an initial draft of your own five stage marketing system (identified above). Determine at least three *conscious focused actions* you will take in each stage. Then begin to execute them during the next twenty-four hours.

Conscious Focused Action Model

This is the thirteenth version of the foundational model, which is found in Chapter 2, *Formula for Creating Wealth*.

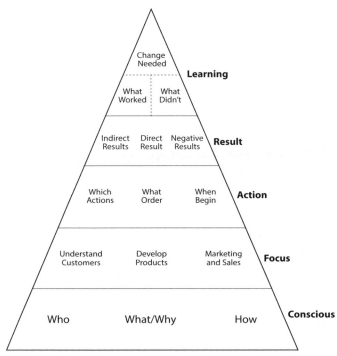

CONSCIOUS FOCUSED ACTION MODEL - 13

The conscious level and focus level interrelate by utilizing each of the words on the conscious level with each focal point on the focus level. *For example*: Utilizing "marketing and sales" from the focus level, ask:

- "What result will *marketing and sales* help achieve?" and, "Why is using *marketing and sales* to accomplish this result a priority?"

- "Who will benefit from using *marketing and sales* to achieve this result?" and, "Who will help use *marketing and sales* to attain this result?"

- "How can I best utilize *marketing and sales* to reach this result?"

Approach the other three levels—action, result, and learning—the same as in the foundational model. If you don't fully achieve your desired result, want to improve your process, or care to achieve your result at a higher level, then iterate. Review each level to determine what needs to change. Return to the conscious level and make the changes as you go through the model again. Then *test* the changes to determine if they are actually better.

CONSCIOUS MILLIONAIRE COACHING

Build Your Strategy

Open your *Conscious Millionaire Journal*. Write a three-step business strategy using *conscious focused action*. Develop your strategy utilizing the concept provided in the *conscious* step below. It is an important concept from this chapter.

   1. Conscious: Marketing leads to sales and sales lead to profits and business growth. Develop a goal of increasing your sales. *For example:* "Increase marketing traffic and convert 20 percent more prospects to buyers each quarter."

   2. Focused: As you focus on your goal, choose three actions that will help you begin to achieve it. Determine the precise order for your actions.

   3. Action: During the next twenty-four hours, execute by taking your three actions.

Grow Your Business

In your *Conscious Millionaire Journal* make notes on how you utilize each of the following to grow your business:

   • Develop a solution to a problem you identified as important to your customer. What is one product you could sell that would solve their problem?

continued

- Identify five ways you could get your customers' attention. Select one and take at least three *conscious focused actions* to implement it this week.

- Write one marketing statement designed to attract your prospect's attention. Test it on prospects to determine how well it works. How many people chose to buy?

Create Your Journey

Here are three choices for what to read next. The first is to read another *conscious* section. The second is to read another *millionaire* section. The third choice is to *journey* through the book linearly, reading it chapter by chapter.

 Conscious: You may want to review "The New Wealth Consciousness" section in Chapter 3, *Win by Becoming Conscious*, before continuing to the next chapter.

 Millionaire: Consider reviewing the "Conscious Millionaire Daily Plan" section in Chapter 6, *Maximize your Results Daily*, before going to the next chapter.

 Journey: Continue forward to Chapter 14, *Create Your Millionaire Journey*.

QR Codes / Links

 Go to the membership site and view a coaching video about how to create high-demand products. As an added bonus, download a copy of the steps for creating your products. Access the site now at:
ConsciousMillionaire.com/member

CREATE YOUR MILLIONAIRE PLAN

Conscious Millionaires
develop a plan and execute quickly!

Unlike many entrepreneurs who have vaguely defined goals and poorly developed plans for attaining them, by applying what you learn in this chapter, you will craft precise goals and build a one-year success plan for achieving them. You will discover how to design goals and develop *Conscious Millionaire Motivation*™. By integrating your visionary purpose into your plan, you will be on track to grow your own Conscious Millionaire Business. Then, you are ready to execute. Finally, you will utilize the *Conscious Focused Action Model* to move forward on your Conscious Millionaire Journey.

HOW TO ACHIEVE BIG GOALS

Most people think of goals as something they *hope* to reach. This is one of the reasons most people fail to reach them.

However, Conscious Millionaires view goals as results they are *committed* to achieving.

When you think of them in this way, goals take on an entirely different meaning. When you say "I am fully *committed* to achieving my goal!" instead of "I *hope* that I achieve it," how much more determined do you feel?

Conscious Millionaires are committed to results. That's why they make bigger differences and grow bigger businesses. It is also why they set and achieve bigger goals. They not only believe in their business purpose, they are passionately committed to achieving it.

Commitment
turns goals into results.

This is my three-step formula for achieving any goal: *what*, *why*, and *how*. Each step has an important purpose:

1. What: The purpose of this step is to dream big and *define* what you want. Until you know what you want, you can't achieve it. If your success were guaranteed, what goals would choose? In this chapter, you'll develop three powerful goals that you can use to guide your business throughout the next year.

2. Why: The purpose of this step is to become massively *motivated*. Develop a list of emotionally charged reasons you want to attain your goal as well as negative consequences that will occur if you don't. In this chapter, you will learn how to develop *Conscious Millionaire Motivation* for each of your goals.

3. How: The purpose of this action is to *plan* how to achieve your goal. Develop "milestone" goals on the way to your major goals, then list the actions you will take. In this chapter, you will develop your one-year goals and success plan for your business.

Here is the *big secret* for using this three-step formula. Think of this formula as being a recipe. As with any process, you must execute these steps in a *specific order*.

For example: When you are at step one, what you want, keep your mind focused on this step instead of wondering how you will achieve the goal. If you jump to step three while you are still dreaming and envisioning what you want, you will cut your vision short, which will result in smaller goals.

> Conscious Millionaires are committed to results. That's why they make bigger differences and grow bigger businesses.

Once you have completed step one, generate reasons *why* it is important for you to achieve your goal. Only after you have completed the why step should you focus on *how* you will accomplish it. As you ponder how you will reach your goal, allow time to generate a wide range of strategies. Look at the goal from multiple angles. Develop what feels like an exhaustive list of ways to reach your goal.

If after completing your list of strategies, you are convinced the goal can *not* be attained, at least not within the established time frame, then return to the first step and make any needed adjustments to your goal—such as "chunksize" or time.

Envision Your Amazing Future

It is time for you to take that vision you created in Chapter 1, *Your Millionaire Journey*, and expand it exponentially. It is time for you to open your mind, allow in more options, and consider what you would do if you knew with *absolute certainty* that your success was guaranteed.

How much bigger would you dare to dream? How much larger would you create your goals? How much bigger results would you achieve?

It's time to turn your big
dreams into your millionaire future.

As you continue to dream of the businesses you want to start and grow, the lives you want to touch, the change you are on Earth to make, it's time for you and I to have a heart-to-heart conversation. It's just the two of us, you and me. No one else is listening. So, let's talk about the reason you picked up this book.

I believe it's because there are hopes and dreams inside of you that need to be let out. There is something major that is still left for you to accomplish, something that will change others and fulfill you.

Your life has brought you to this precise moment. The tumblers in the universe have all come into alignment. You have come face-to-face with your destiny. That destiny is to be of service to humanity.

This, my friend, is why you picked up this book. You are ready to grow your business into a profitable force that gives important value to your customers. You are ready to break through your comfort zone and develop a massive vision of what you want to accomplish. You are ready to achieve, give, and live at levels you may have thought impossible only yesterday.

Consider these questions: Do you want to make a difference on a grand scale? Do you want to grow your business exponentially? Would you like to have the money, resources, and time off so you can enjoy an amazing lifestyle, provide for your family, create a great future for your children, and be in a position to support causes you care about?

If your answer is yes, then you are ready to take your business and life to new levels. You are ready to stop holding back and start dreaming big. You are ready to act with bold conviction by choosing big goals that inspire you to take action.

Now, what would happen if you became fully committed to multiplying your results over the next three years? How much more could you accomplish?

Would it be twice as much? Three times as much? Four times, seven times, even ten times as much as you originally conceived? How much larger vision could you bring to life?

You are ready to create a big, expansive vision of your dream business, achievable in three years. What does it look, feel, and sound like? What are your products and services? How big are your revenues and profits? Who are your primary customers? What do you most enjoy doing every day? How has your life changed?

> You have come face-to-face with your destiny. That destiny is to be of service to humanity.

Continue to dream big. In the next section, you will develop the goals that will guide your business for the next three years.

> **Coaching:** Open your *Conscious Millionaire Journal*. Focus your mind on building your ideal business in three years. Write a description of your ideal business that includes: what it looks like, the sounds that occur at work, and how you will feel after you fully achieve your vision.

GOALS GUIDE YOU INTO YOUR FUTURE

By reading *Conscious Millionaire*, you have learned there are infinite opportunities and abundant wealth available to you. However, in order for you to act upon these opportunities, you must develop goals that can guide your business into the future. It's time to select the goals for your business. There are three types of goals: *purpose, financial,* and *business critical.*

Develop a three-year goal for each type:

1. Purpose Goal: expresses how you will turn your visionary purpose into products and services that *transform* your customer.

2. Financial Goal: your revenue, profit, or other specific financial outcome you target for any period of time.

3. Mission Critical Goal: a specific goal that is critical to your business success. If you want to build a high-growth business, then you must achieve "escape velocity." This means doubling your business every one to three years. *Note*: this term comes from the space industry. The majority of the fuel that a rocket carries is utilized to escape the gravitational pull of earth. All businesses face the same issue—getting past everything that consumes your energy and pulls you down.

Four of the factors that help to attain velocity growth are: marketing/sales, systems automation, product creation, and team development. Until you achieve escape velocity, it should be your *mission critical goal.* After you attain it, each year make your third goal something that is critical to your continued growth. *For example*: Focus on any of the nine keys of your business model, an important project, or a growth initiative, such as expanding into a new region or market.

> If you want to build a high-growth business, then you must achieve "escape velocity."

The first two types of goals, *purpose* and *financial*, are of equal importance. Further, they are mutually intertwined and complement one another. Neither goal can be fully accomplished without also achieving the other. This is why the *dual focus* of your Conscious Millionaire business is your purpose and financial goals.

For example: By developing products and services that transform your customer, you attract more customers, make more sales, and increase profits. By having more financial resources, you are in a position to develop more products, expand your marketing, and help more customers.

> **Coaching:** Open your *Conscious Millionaire Journal*. Write each of your three-year goals—one for each type of goal: purpose, financial, mission critical. Determine the specific milestone your business must achieve within twelve months in order to reach each of the three-year goals. Turn these twelve-month milestones into your one-year goals.

Conscious Millionaire Motivation

Once you have a clearly defined and well-written goal—the "what" step in the goal formula—turn your attention to the "why" step. Recall the purpose of this step, which is to assure that your level of motivation to achieve your goal will propel you forward so you easily move past any internal or external obstacle.

Goals that motivate you, act like magnets. They pull you toward them. You feel drawn to reach them. They lift you up and make you feel excited. By contrast, goals that don't motivate, act like weights that pull you down. They drain you and literally pull the life energy out of you.

If you want to become a Conscious Millionaire, you can't afford to waste your time, money, and resources attempting to achieve goals you honestly don't want or care about.

Only choose goals
that deeply motivate you!

When you think of the three goals you have chosen, do you instantly feel 100 percent motivated to take any action needed to achieve them? Make a quick list in your mind of things that could easily stop you. These could include: you didn't get enough sleep, so you don't feel like working hard; other people ridicule you for having such big goals; friends want you to spend more time with them. Develop enough motivation so you can quickly blast through any obstacles or distractions.

Here are three possible reasons *why* you aren't motivated:

1. You haven't tapped into *enough* emotional reasons for achieving it;

2. You must go too far outside your comfort zone to achieve the goal;

3. You choose the goal for the wrong reason, such as you feel you "should" do it or you are attempting to "please someone else" at the expense of pleasing yourself.

Now that you understand this, *consciously choosing* goals that are both right for you and highly *motivate* you is easy. Only choose goals you really want, ones that excite you and feel authentic to you. Then develop a list of emotionally-charged benefits for attaining them and emotionally-charged costs of failing.

One of the major limitations of most motivational approaches is they only provide one or two ways to become motivated—the benefits/costs to *you* in the present, and possibly to you in the future. However, *Conscious Millionaire Motivation* is significantly more robust and effective because it provides six ways to become highly motivated.

These six dimensions are the benefits of succeeding and costs of failing to *you*, *others*, and *society/community*—both *now* and in the *future*.

	You	Others	Society
Now	gains & costs with level 10 feelings	gains & costs with level 10 feelings	gains & costs with level 10 feelings
Future	gains & costs with level 10 feelings	gains & costs with level 10 feelings	gains & costs with level 10 feelings

In this diagram, "you" refers to you or your business; "others" refers to a specific person or type of person, such as your partner, children, or customers; and "society" refers to a larger group, geographical area, or community, such as the people who live near you.

Define your "now" time dimension as starting today and extending until the date you plan to complete your goal. Define your "future" as beginning immediately after this goal is complete.

Note: When developing motivation for your one-year and three-year business goals, define the

> Think of benefits and costs as outcomes that are emotionally charged for you.

present as today through one year (your one-year goals) and the future as running from one to three years (your three-year goals).

Consider the effect that achieving, or failing to achieve, your one-year goals would have on your ability to reach your three-year goals.

In each of these six dimensions, develop two lists. The first list contains your emotionally-charged benefits of reaching your goals. The second list is comprised of your emotionally-charged costs of failing to reach the goals. Think of benefits and costs as outcomes that are emotionally charged for you.

For instance, you passionately desire benefits. You look forward to experiencing the intense positive feelings that you associate with them. These may include joy, peace, happiness, fulfillment, or pride of accomplishment.

By contrast, even the thought of enduring the *costs* of failing may arouse deep negative feelings within you. These could include fear, embarrassment, humiliation, or other equally negative feelings about failing or not succeeding.

I refer to these as your "level 10 feelings"—your emotions that get you totally motivated. Think of them as the strongest feelings you typically experience. Intense positive feelings are your *positive level 10s* and intense negative feelings are your *negative level 10s*.

> **Coaching:** Open your *Conscious Millionaire Journal*. Sketch the two-by-three motivation grid found in this section. Then complete it for each of your three-year business goals you developed in the previous section.

Your One-Year Success Plan

Your success plan translates your one-year goals—*purpose, financial,* and *mission critical*—into milestone goals (think of these as quarterly goals) and actions for achieving them. For you to turn your plan into results, you must completely *believe* your plan is achievable. In your gut—you need to feel it is the *right plan* for your business over the next year.

Now, in order to develop a success plan, first review the business model you developed in Chapter 12, *Develop Your*

Business Model. Refine it one more time by asking people on your team, your business coach, or mastermind group, for input.

Second, review both the three-year and one-year goals you developed earlier in this chapter. Make any shifts that you believe necessary so they completely reflect what you want, and you feel 100 percent motivated to achieve them!

> For you to turn your plan into results, you must completely *believe* your plan is achievable

Third, develop your one-year success plan by utilizing the following format. Why is a success plan important? There are three reasons:

1. It gives a direction for your business by defining three specific goals for the next year.

2. It defines the milestone goals and actions necessary to rapidly grow your business.

3. It provides a process for continually testing and revising your business model—for constantly improving your model—throughout the year.

As you put your success plan into action, you will discover which of the assumptions in your business model are accurate, and which ones need to change. During the course of twelve months, you will likely make many changes in both your model and plan as you respond to feedback from your market.

The key to a great success plan is to establish well-defined one-year goals that provide you with a clear direction, while remaining flexible as to how you achieve them.

Because you want to step onto a fast-growth path, make a commitment to complete your business model and success plan in the next seven days. If you take *conscious focused action*, you not only can, but you will, complete your model and plan. Then seven days from now, you will be ready to put them into action.

There are only seven steps to your success plan. They are designed to help you maintain *awareness of your one-year goals* while staying *focused on today's actions*.

1. Introduction: Your introduction has five parts. Write concise statements that should be clear to anyone who reads your plan. Note that some of this information, such as visionary purpose, niche market, and products, come from your business model. Your introduction consists of:

a. Business Name, Location, Visionary Purpose: Begin your success plan with your business name, location, and statement of purpose.

b. One-Year Goals: Choose three one-year goals that will move you toward your three-year vision for your business. View these goals as interrelated and having equal importance. They are:

1. Purpose Goal: how you will transform your customer, such as developing or updating a product;

2. Financial Goal: the revenue, cash-flow, and profit you want to achieve; and

3. Mission Critical Goal: a specific goal that is critical to your one-year success.

Get started
and stay focused.

c. Current Team Members: Write one short paragraph about each current team member with their name, responsibilities, major skills, relevant prior experience, and education. Include coaches, mentors, and advisors. State how each member will help you grow your business and achieve your goals.

d. Niche Market: Describe your specific market(s) and customer avatar.

e. Products: List your current products and services as well as price points. Also list new products and services you intend to offer in the next year and initial test price points. Include any upgrades to existing products and services.

2. Current Quarter "Milestone-Goals": Each quarter, choose one or more goals that support achieving *each of your top three goals* for the year. These milestones represent your projected achievements for that quarter. At the beginning of the third month of each quarter, start to formulate milestone-goals for the next quarter.

3. Current Month Goals: Translate your current quarter goals into current month goals. You will focus on these monthly milestones during the next thirty days. In the final week of the current month, establish goals for the next month based upon the current month's achievements and what needs to occur next in order to meet your quarterly goals.

4. Action Strategies: Identify which action steps are necessary to achieve your goals for any time period. To turn these actions into a strategy, arrange them in a specific sequence, or order, in which they should occur. Recall the strategy exercise at the end of each chapter: use the *conscious focused action* sequence to develop strategies.

5. Review & Revision: There are five levels of reviews, and they naturally flow into one another. They are daily, weekly, monthly, quarterly and annually.

a. Daily: At the end of the day, review your achievements. Develop your next day plan utilizing the "Conscious Millionaire Daily Plan" which is found in Chapter 6, *Maximize Your Success Daily*.

b. Weekly: At the end of each week, review your key financial metrics which measure how well you are achieving your financial goals. Then make any needed revisions in your objectives for the next week. Healthy business growth will always be reflected in your financial metrics. These include: revenues, cash-flow, gross profits, bottom-line profits, as well as the costs and time required to convert leads into buying customers and make additional sales to your current customers.

c. Monthly: At the end of each month, review the results you achieved for each of your goals as well as your key financial metrics (see above), including your cash-flow statement. This will determine your level of success and any areas in which you need to make changes. Establish your goals for the next month. *Note*: An important way to measure how well you are achieving your purpose goal is whether your revenues and profits are growing; that is, whether customers are choosing to make purchases.

d. Quarterly: At the end of the quarter, allow two days for review. On the first day, perform a typical "monthly" review as outlined above with the addition of establishing goals for the next quarter (including the first month of that quarter). On the second day, allow time to reflect so ideas and insights arise into your consciousness.

Consider how you can better serve your customers and how you can increase your revenues and profits. What are you not selling your customers that would benefit them? Ideally, take this second day of reflection by yourself. Choose a setting that helps you connect with a higher consciousness and visionary state; this is discussed in Chapter 3, *Win by Becoming Conscious.*

e. Annual: At the end of the year, conduct both a quarterly and annual review at the same time. If you rely on several key team members, consider organizing a CEO retreat. You may want to also include your business coach, mentors, or advisors at your meetings or retreat. Follow the quarterly review and revision with the addition of the following: develop new three-year goals so you roll your three-year vision out a year. Then select your one-year goals for your next twelve months.

6. Desired Team Members: Now that you know what you want to accomplish, make a list of the skills needed for your team. Next, list both your skills as an entrepreneur as well as those of any *current* team members, which include outsourced people. Remove these skills from the list of what you *need*; the skills that remain on the list are what you still need to acquire in order to have a robust team. You may want to combine these skills to form one or more new team positions. Another option, which may prove far more economical, is to outsource work that requires specialized skills on a part-time, as-needed, basis. *For example*: building and maintaining websites, design work, video editing, or social media marketing.

7. Three-Year Cash-Flow Pro Forma: In order to know if your business plans make financial sense, you need to create three years of Cash-Flow Pro Forma. The first year should be monthly and the next two years, quarterly. Your Pro Forma projects your *cash in* (money received) and *cash out* (money paid). The most useful way to think of your cash-flow projections is as a *feasibility study* to determine your likelihood of success.

You want to discover if, based upon reasonable assumptions, your current business model and success plan will provide the *level* of cash needed on the specific *dates* you will need it (such as when you pay for products or future bills), so you will be able to stay in business and grow your business. Your Pro Forma helps you determine if you should make adjustments in your model or assumptions upfront, instead of finding out the hard way by losing money.

For example: A business can be highly profitable on paper (actual booked profits) and still go out of business if you lack the money to pay your bills and keep your organization running. How can this happen? You make a large number of sales and must pay suppliers this week. But, your customers are not required to pay you for another thirty days. Therefore, you don't have the cash in the bank to keep operating.

Both during the initial stage of developing your business model and success plan, as well as during your regular scheduled reviews, discuss results for each of the three major goals with a coach, mentor, or other trusted advisor. An objective set of eyes that are not directly involved with your day-to-day operations will help you make better decisions—including the adjustments to make as your business grows.

> **Coaching:** Open your *Conscious Millionaire Journal*. This is an advanced coaching; it is my personal challenge to you. Because you have journeyed this far, you are ready. Replace all the "goals" in your success plan with a new label. Call them "results." Instead of seeing them as goals you *hope* to reach, think of them as results you are *committed* to achieving. Feel the difference! Take the challenge! Create the Results!

Conscious Focused Action Model

This is the fourteenth version of the foundational model, which is found in Chapter 2, *Formula for Creating Wealth*.

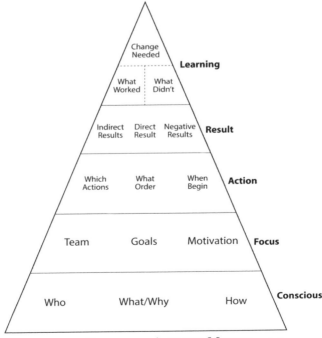

Conscious Focused Action Model - 14

The conscious level and focus level interrelate by utilizing each of the words on the conscious level with each focal point on the focus level. *For example*: Utilizing "motivation" from the focus level, ask:

- "What result will my becoming *motivated* help achieve?" and, "Why is my becoming *motivated* to accomplish this result a priority?"

- "Who will benefit from my becoming *motivated* to achieve this result?" and, "Who will help me stay *motivated* to attain this result?"

- "How can I best utilize my *motivation* to reach this result?"

Approach the other three levels—action, result, and learning—the same as in the foundational model. If you don't fully achieve your desired result, want to improve your process, or care to achieve your result at a higher level, then iterate. Review each level to determine what needs to change. Return to the conscious level and make the changes as you go through the model again. Then *test* the changes to determine if they are actually better.

Your Conscious Millionaire Journey

Think back to the beginning of this book and how you defined what your ideal life and business would look like in three years. That was before you read *Conscious Millionaire* and considered all the possibilities available to you. Moreover, it was prior to you developing *New Wealth Consciousness*—which includes you, others, and society all winning together.

When you began this book, you had not learned of the *Formula for Creating Wealth* and *Conscious Focused Action Models*. Therefore, you didn't have these to help you achieve your goals and build wealth.

You had not yet learned of *Millionaire Inner Zone* and how, by entering your *flow-zone*, you rapidly attract the resources, people, solutions, and opportunities you need. Also, you had not learned how to enter your *focus-zone* to achieve results quickly.

> Move forward with absolute confidence and certainty that you can create meaningful change on a grand scale.

As you began to take what you learned and put it into *conscious focused action*, you expanded your thoughts of what you are capable of achieving. You realized we each have a calling, a reason for being on earth. By developing a picture of your true north, the difference you want to make, you became more aware of your personal calling.

As you developed an understanding of what it means to become a *conscious leader*, you discovered how to translate your true north into a visionary business purpose.

You learned how to multiply your results and which new habits will help you become a Conscious Millionaire. Next, you pondered what it means to live in abundance. You began to shift your limiting money beliefs into new empowering beliefs; you freed your mind of old, scarcity beliefs that limited you in the past.

You discovered what it means to live with integrity, how to build powerful relationships, and the three uses of money: to pay for your lifestyle, invest for the future, and give back to others. You learned how to create your customer avatar and develop products your customers will eagerly purchase.

By reading *Conscious Millionaire*, completing the coaching, and utilizing the resources provided on your membership site, you have significantly increased your capacity to grow your business. You are now prepared to develop your new business model and one-year success plan.

At this very moment, you are ready to let go of any fear that has held you back; shed every doubt that may have previously kept you from taking action; discard any negative thoughts that in the past may have blocked you from fully believing in yourself. It is time for you to let go of everything that may have hindered you in the past.

> There is a passionate difference you want to make, a deeper purpose you have yet to fully achieve.

You are ready to let go for one specific reason. Your time has come. It's time for you to move forward with absolute confidence and certainty that you can create meaningful change on a grand scale.

It is why you are here on Earth. There is a difference you want to make, a deeper purpose you have yet to achieve. Think of this as the legacy you were born to create.

Your path for accomplishing this is building a highly profitable and purposeful business—one that changes others' lives and our world. This is your destiny. It is the reason you picked up *Conscious Millionaire*.

Now, imagine accomplishing 10 times, 100 times, even 1,000 times or more your current level of success and contribution. Because that, my friend, is your true potential.

It doesn't matter if you already are a successful entrepreneur or still have the dream of owning your first business. It doesn't matter if you are young, middle aged, or just looking for a new direction. Your time is now. Congratulations for taking the first steps to becoming a Conscious Millionaire.

However, the journey has just begun. As a member of the Conscious Millionaire Community, you have the path, a complete set of tools, and the support needed to build and grow your business consciously.

Now you have come to your decision point. Will you continue at your current pace, or will you make your decision today to enter a new stage and achieve escape velocity? It's time, and you feel it to the core of your being.

This is why I personally invite you to step up and say...

> *"Yes! Count me in.*
> *I want to make my difference.*
> *I am ready to bring my message forward.*
> *I seek to grow my business consciously.*
> *I now join the ranks of those committed*
> *to becoming Conscious Millionaires!"*

It's the right decision for you and your family; for your customers and your team; and for our society and global community. It's time for you to step up and play big.

You have my support, the support of my team, and the support of all the other like-minded entrepreneurs who are part of this growing world-wide community.

Following this chapter is a section titled *Personal Message from J V*. In it, I tell you about a special gift that I have for you, a FREE program. The program shows you how to develop the *Mindset to Make Millions* and create wealth consciously.

I am excited for you and your future, for the life you are now ready to live, for the business you are ready to build, and for the vision you are ready to bring to our world.

Welcome to YOUR Conscious Millionaire Journey!

CONSCIOUS MILLIONAIRE COACHING

Build Your Strategy

Open your *Conscious Millionaire Journal*. Write a three-step business strategy using *conscious focused action*. Develop your strategy utilizing the concept provided in the *conscious* step below. It is an important concept from this chapter.

1. Conscious: Throughout this book, the primary focus has been on your Journey. However, it is intertwined with the lives and journeys of everyone else on your team. Create a goal of helping each team member excel. *For example*: "Each person on my team will be mentored once a week to help them improve their skills."

2. Focused: As you focus on your goal, choose three actions that will help you begin to achieve it. Determine the precise order for your actions.

3. Action: During the next twenty-four hours, execute by taking your three actions.

Grow Your Business

In your *Conscious Millionaire Journal* make notes on how you utilize each of the following to grow your business:

- On what date will you become a Conscious Millionaire? If you are already a financial millionaire, on what date will you make your next million?

- How many customers will your business help over the next three years?

- Ask one successful business person you know to review your success plan. Discuss any changes they recommend. Make the changes that feel right to you.

Create Your Journey

Here are three choices for what to read next. The first is to read another *conscious* section. The second is to read another *millionaire* section. The third choice is to *journey* through the book linearly, reading it chapter by chapter.

Conscious: You may want to review the "Your Ideal Life and Business" section in Chapter 1, *Your Millionaire Journey*, because it is relevant to the material in this chapter.

Millionaire: Consider reviewing "Conscious Millionaire Confidence" section in Chapter 6, *Maximize Your Results Daily*, as it will help you to achieve big goals.

Journey: Continue on your journey to the "Personal Message from J V" which includes information on a *free* program: *Mindset to Make Millions!*

QR Codes / Links

Go to the membership site and view a coaching video about how to achieve *Conscious Millionaire Motivation*. As a bonus, download a copy of the *Conscious Millionaire Motivation* model. Access the site now at: **ConsciousMillionaire.com/member**

Personal Message
From J V

Congratulations for beginning your Conscious Millionaire Journey! I consider it an honor that you read my book. I wrote it for people like you: entrepreneurs who aspire to make a powerful difference both through their business and life.

As the Founder of Conscious Millionaire Institute LLC, my goal is to provide you with the path, tools, and support needed to grow—personally and as an entrepreneur. When you grow as a person, you will expand your ability to both grow your business and make a powerful contribution to our world.

By choosing the Conscious Millionaire path, you join a community of like-minded people who are dedicated to evolving their consciousness. Whether you are currently an entrepreneur or seek to start a new business, you can become a role model of what it means to consciously create financial success.

By taking a conscious approach to business, you demonstrate to your customers, employees, outsourced support staff, business associates, as well as family and friends, how to create wealth without sacrificing your values or integrity.

The world needs you to take your place as a conscious leader. By employing people who share a heart-felt connection with your values and purpose, you expand the consciousness of what is possible—for individuals, for businesses, and for our society as a whole.

By following the guidance in this book, you've completed your first milestone on your Conscious Millionaire Journey. Now, it is time for you to complete your *next milestone* by developing or revising your business model, selecting your one-year goals, and creating your one-year success plan.

Whether you are an established entrepreneur or want to start your first business, creating the right business model, goals, and plan is the next step on your path to growing your business. That seems like a daunting task for many people. Yet, it doesn't need to be.

You can accomplish all of this in as little as seven days. To help you achieve this, I am providing you with a FREE program, *Mindset to Make Millions*! Discover how to consciously create wealth and enjoy a life of total abundance.

The program is designed for entrepreneurs who desire to take a conscious path for growing their businesses. They want to develop their wealth mindset so they can both make millions and make an important contribution to our world. Sign-up now by using either the *QR Code* or link below.

I look forward to you attending the program and hearing about your results!

Make Your Difference,
JV CRUM III, Founder/CEO
Conscious Millionaire Institute LLC

To sign-up for the next online program, *Mindset to Make Millions*, use this link now:
ConsciousMillionaire.com/mindset

About the Author

J V Crum III became a self-made millionaire in his twenties. He is an entrepreneur, investor, mentor, visionary strategist, and Founder/CEO of Conscious Millionaire Institute LLC, a global entrepreneur training, coaching, and wealth product business.

The Institute's programs help both start-up and established entrepreneurs achieve their higher purpose and create higher profits. He is a speaker on entrepreneurial success, conscious business, and youth leadership.

As the Founder/Director of Conscious World Foundation Inc., a 501c(3) non-profit, J V oversees the development of its youth programs. Conscious World Foundation provides global youth leadership training and annually produces Conscious World Day.

Its mission is to develop the next generation of conscious global leaders—thereby raising the consciousness of humanity worldwide. All of its programs are based on his *Triple Win* principle: you, others, and society winning together.

J V holds three graduate degrees. He is a licensed attorney, JD; holds a Masters in Business Administration, MBA; and earned a MS in Psychology. He also has more than three decades of experience in the human potential community and is a leader in the consciousness movement.

As a man influenced by both Western and Eastern spiritual traditions and practices, J V believes in the Divine interplay in life and business. His personal motto is "trust perfect timing."

He loves the outdoors, nature, and all things related to water, from class-five water rafting to skiing, scuba diving, and camping near mountain streams.

J V is an avid lover of the arts, including many forms of music, ranging from jazz, blues, folk, and Indie bands to rock, opera, and classical. He also enjoys food, wine, cooking, and pursues a health-focused lifestyle.

A world traveler, one of his personal goals is to become a member of the Travelers' Century Club, by visiting at least one hundred countries around the world.

J V Crum iii, Speaker

J V Crum III speaks to business groups, organizations, and companies. His topics include entrepreneur success, business growth, and becoming a socially-conscious business by combining a profit motive with achieving a higher purpose. His entertaining speaking style connects with audiences in an authentic way that both inspires and moves them to action.

The focus of his speaking is the Conscious Millionaire path to wealth building, business success, and making a difference. He can also be booked as a guest on radio, TV, podcasts, webinars and for conference breakout sessions and panels.

Additionally, as Director of the Conscious World Foundation, the youth leadership non-profit he founded, J V speaks to youth groups. He enjoys speaking at high-schools and colleges as well as to youth leaders. Topics include: personal and financial success, your life as a journey, becoming a conscious leader, and giving back to make our world better.

To learn more visit:
ConsciousMillionaire.com
Email: speaking@ConsciousMillionaire.com
Call in U.S: 1-800-489-9496

ACKNOWLEDGMENTS

This has been an amazing journey of finding my voice and learning how to express it. Without the support of many people who provided their talents and personal encouragement to help me complete this project, you wouldn't be reading *Conscious Millionaire*. My heartfelt appreciation goes to each one of them.

I am grateful to my amazing editor, LinDee Rochelle. Thanks for being there to answer my endless phone calls and provide constant advice on how best to express my ideas. Every writer should be so fortunate as to have an editor who mirrors their voice.

To my longtime friend, Kevin Schoeninger, who is a great writer himself, I give my deepest thanks for supporting me in the development of my voice. Judith Briles, a mentor as well as consultant deserves thanks for believing in me. Likewise, I appreciate the final book review by John Maling.

My thanks to Rebecca Finkel for *Conscious Millionaire's* interior design. I want to acknowledge Bob Thompson for my author photo, and Amy Collins for consulting on marketing and book placement. I also appreciate the early assistance of Jared Kuritz.

There were scores of people who took time to engage in conversation, read early drafts, and share their insights with me. Without them, the book, *Conscious Millionaire*, wouldn't be half the quality. My deep gratitude for their contributions. I want to especially thank two close friends whose thoughts I always value, Gail Sauer and Linda Norman.

I deeply appreciate Dame D C Cordova, a thought-leader in the consciousness and business movement, for her friendship, and honoring me by writing the book's Foreword. You are a beacon who is shining the way forward for the new socially conscious entrepreneur.

Hazel Henderson, founder of *EthicalMarkets*, thank you for becoming a friend, mentor, and guide. You helped me develop a deeper understanding of conscious approaches to commerce and business. And, Rosalinda Sanquiche, Executive Director of Ethical Markets, your comments and input were invaluable.

Gary Ryan Blair, thanks for your mentorship, guidance, and insights on how to best develop the book as well as programs at Conscious Millionaire Institute. Quincy Ellis, I deeply appreciate for your wisdom, insights, and our discussions that helped me refine many of the book's concepts.

To my cousin, Nancy Garrett, a gifted teacher and loyal friend, my thanks for our discussions on how to provide the greatest value to readers.

A note of gratitude, too, for those with whom I've had other important discussions or who read my manuscript and provided significant comments: Gloria Flora, Hal Pitt, Scot Laney, Kathy Browne, Ricki Smith, Dana Curtis, Pat Martin, Marc Imhoff, Bret Temple, Joyce Cotton, Esther Castor, Aaron Campo, Jeanne House, Greg Snider, Anne Salisbury, Greg Meyerhoff, Dion Cini, Dave Fechtman, Melissa Valenti, Bill Park, David Goberville, and Tim Husted.

I also want to thank all of the other entrepreneurs and leaders who are also pioneering conscious approaches to business. Through our efforts, we can revolutionize entrepreneurship into an experience in which we can all win together.

Conscious Millionaire
Membership

Because you are a reader of Conscious Millionaire, I am providing you with 30 days FREE access to our Conscious Millionaire Membership Site. Our membership community is a group of like-minded conscious entrepreneurs who care about one another and our world. They are people like you who want to create wealth by helping others and our world.

As a member, you receive access to resources such as videos and downloads that enhance your experience of reading this book. You also have access to monthly Expert Interviews, Training Calls, and our Millionaire Blog. Additionally, you receive advance information on new programs as well as special member only bonuses when we launch new trainings and products.

Each month is a new topic, such as getting started, mindset, goals, and strategies. Think of your membership as a monthly program designed to help you grow your business, increase wealth, and make a bigger difference.

Our entire team and I are invested in your success. As a member you will find support, tools, and like-minded entrepreneurs. I look forward to speaking with you on our Training Calls.

To access your 30 days FREE membership go to this link now: **ConsciousMillionaire.com/member**

Conscious Millionaire
Masterminds

Napoleon Hill, in his book *Think and Grow Rich*, defined mastermind as the organized effort of two or more people to achieve a goal by working in harmony with one another. Through participation in a *Conscious Millionaire Mastermind* group, you share knowledge, experience, and insight, while also sharing a visionary consciousness with like-minded entrepreneurs.

By entering your zone and sharing a group consciousness, the participants in a mastermind rapidly become more productive. You share positive energy and contribute to your group's creative mindset. Together, you innovate, expand one another's possibilities, and help each other discover new opportunities. You achieve far more than you could alone.

Conscious Millionaire Masterminds is a group of people with a common goal of building financial wealth by making a visionary difference. Participants use the formula, principles and tools in this book for the common good of everyone in the group. And by collaborating, you will expand your consciousness, evolve your ideas, and develop better solutions for how you build wealth by contributing to our world.

Another important benefit of a mastermind opportunity is that the other people in your group will see your business model, products, services, and wealth opportunities through different lenses. This is because they have varying perspectives and can offer valuable insights that are based upon their unique experiences.

It is also why you will see their business and opportunities differently than they will, and can therefore offer fresh insights to help them grow their businesses.

Conscious Millionaire Masterminds
help participants evolve consciously and financially.

Each participant will learn what is, and is not, working for their business. You can also leverage each another's experiences, knowledge, and resources into greater success. Further, you will expand your vision of what is possible for you.

If you came together with other entrepreneurs who are also dedicated to delivering products that make life on this planet better, how would your business and life change? How much more motivated and inspired might you become? How much more could you accomplish?

What other benefits would you receive? Would you refine your business vision, discover new opportunities for money, or create insights for new products? Would you achieve your goals two, five, ten times faster by sharing resources and tapping into one another's circles of influence?

I personally invite you to contact us today to discuss *Conscious Millionaire Masterminds*. Join with other entrepreneurs who want to consciously create their wealth by making an important contribution to others and our world. Call or email to learn more about our application process and how our masterminds can benefit you. To learn more visit:

 ConsciousMillionaire.com

Or email: **mastermind@ConsciousMillionaire.com**

Conscious World Foundation, Inc.

The Conscious World Foundation, Inc., is a 501c(3) non-profit organization. It supports our Conscious World Youth Training programs that will expand globally with the goal of working with youth in more than 160 countries. Our intent is to help create the next generation of worldwide conscious leaders.

The flagship program works with youth organizations. We help youth from age six through college identify a specific difference they want to create in their community. Then, by utilizing our process, they develop and implement their group project.

Through these trainings, youth learn how to achieve individual success, team success, project management and leadership. The program teaches many of the concepts in *Conscious Millionaire*, including the *Triple Win*: you, others, and society all winning together.

The foundation also sponsors the annual Conscious World Day. This is a day to celebrate youth and their potential to lead our future. A portion of *Conscious Millionaire* sales are contributed to the Conscious World Foundation, Inc.

 To learn more please visit:
ConsciousWorld.org